This book is dedicated to all those who suffered during the Second World War.

Nowhere's Child

ABOUT THE CO-WRITER

 Naomi Linehan is a journalist and documentary maker who worked in flagship current affairs and features programmes on Newstalk Radio from 2008-2014. She was born in Dublin and grew up in Zambia. In addition to her radio work, Naomi has written articles for *The Irish Times* and various other newspapers and magazines. *Nowhere's Child* is her first book.

Nowhere's Child

The inspiring story of how one
woman survived Hitler's breeding
camps and found an Irish home

Kari Rosvall

with Naomi Linehan

HACHETTE
BOOKS
IRELAND

First published in Ireland in 2015 by
HACHETTE BOOKS IRELAND

1

Cataloguing in Publication Data is available from the British Library

ISBN 978 1 4736 0947 1

Typeset in Calisto by redrattledesign.com

Printed and bound in Great Britain by CPI Group (UK) Ltd, Croydon, CR0 4YY

Hachette Books Ireland policy is to use papers that are natural, renewable and recyclable products and made from wood grown in sustainable forests. The logging and manufacturing processes are expected to conform to the environmental regulations of the country of origin.

Hachette Books Ireland
8 Castlecourt Centre
Castleknock
Dublin 15, Ireland

A division of Hachette UK Ltd
338 Euston Road, London NW1 3BH
www.hachette.ie

Every reasonable effort has been made to trace copyright holders, but if there are any errors or omissions, Hachette Ireland will be pleased to insert the appropriate acknowledgement in any subsequent printings or editions.

1

The beginning

My name is Kari. I am an ordinary person, except for one thing.

I was born at the age of 64.

I was five foot four inches tall, and weighed 154 pounds. My hair was grey and my hands were old.

Unlike other newborns, I did not cry. There was no one there to mother me, so I was quiet. But I cannot stay quiet.

I do not know how much time I have left, how long or short the rest of my life will be. It is time to tell my story. I will try to tell it as best I can.

All my life people asked me, 'Where were you born?' It's a simple question that I could never answer.

There are two points in everyone's life that are in darkness – the beginning and the end. It is usually a doctor who tells us how our lives will end, and parents who tell us how we began.

But I didn't have parents to shed light on my beginning. I stumbled on that awful truth by accident.

It wasn't until the year 2008, in my 64th year, that I discovered who I really was.

I was part of humanity's darkest secret.

My keepers – I do not know what else to call them – had made sure no one would find out. They decided I would have no mother. They decided I would have no father. I was born to order, a product of their Nazi madness. I would serve one purpose – their purpose.

From me they would make many more, and from the offspring of my offspring, more would come. I had no past, but I would breed the future.

Who knows what I would have done, what I would have become, if I had not escaped.

I got out because they were defeated. But it could have been a very different story, not just for me, but for the world.

This is a horror story. And it is also a love story. It is the story of a child of nowhere – nowhere's child. It is a true story – my story.

I do not know where to begin. Perhaps in 1961, in Linköping, a small town in the south of Sweden. At that time I thought I was just a young girl growing up, ordinary in every way – but nothing could be further from the truth.

2

Linköping, Sweden, 1961

You remember the transitions in your life more than anything else. When you step out of a place of comfort into the unknown. These are frightening times, and at the same time thrilling.

I was shaking as I sat in the corridor. I was the last to be called. The heavy oak door opened, and a woman in a nurse's uniform appeared.

'Kari?'

It was time.

'We're ready for you now,' she said, and gestured for me to follow her.

I had worn my best dress and hoped I looked presentable. I was only 17, and was trying to look older. I had never been to a job interview before.

I followed the nurse into the room, surprised at the weight of the door. I let it go and it slammed shut.

An older woman sat behind a desk. She had an air of authority about her.

She gestured to a chair in the middle of the room.

'Sit down.'

The nurse sat beside her with a notebook in her lap and a pen at the ready.

'My name is Sister Dagmar,' she said, 'and this is Greta.'

She nodded towards the nurse.

My mouth was dry.

'We have your application here. You are Kari Andersson… is that correct?'

'Yes, Kari Andersson.' I took a deep breath to steady my nerves.

'And where do you come from, Kari?' asked Sister Dagmar, peering out at me over her round glasses.

'Malexander. A farm in Malexander. It's just 30 miles from here. Not far.'

'We know where Malexander is,' she said.

'Sorry.'

'And you live there with your parents?'

'With Simon and Valborg.'

'They're your parents?'

'Yes … well … yes.'

Dagmar looked down at the form again. 'So you were born in Malexander?'

'You need to know where I was born?'

'We need your basic details, Kari. You've left out a lot of information in your application. So – birth place? Malexander?'

'No, not in Malexander.'

'Well then, where?'

This was the question I had hoped they wouldn't ask. I mean, what does it matter where you are born? The room was silent. Dagmar leaned forward with her elbows on the desk. She held the application form between her thumb and forefinger.

'I don't know,' I said.

The nurse stopped writing and looked up from her notebook.

'You don't know where you were born?'

This wasn't going well.

'Kari is not a Swedish name,' Dagmar said, as though accusing me of something. 'Where did you get the name Kari?'

'I don't know. I was adopted.'

'Adopted? I thought you said you lived with your parents?'

'Yes, I was adopted when I was three. By Simon and Valborg. I grew up on their farm in Malexander.'

It sounded more like an excuse than a statement of fact. I wondered if it would be better to just leave now.

Dagmar placed the application on the desk and removed her glasses. She rubbed her eyes and gestured towards the nurse to take down my reply. Her eyes looked small without the glasses. The nurse made a note. Dagmar continued to peruse the form.

'You left school at 14, is that right?'

'I'm clever,' I said, without thinking. And then I blushed. 'I just didn't like school.'

Dagmar laughed.

'Yes, well, I suppose we can all understand something of that. But you have worked since leaving school, I see.'

'I've always helped my parents – my adoptive parents – on the farm. Up at dawn every day to milk the cows. I'm used to hard work. And more recently, I've been a child-minder here in Linköping.'

'So, if you were to work here, you wouldn't mind being away from Malexander?'

'I wouldn't mind at all. There's not much to do there, at my age. I climbed trees when I was a child. I loved Malexander, but I'm ready for something new now. Maybe something bigger to climb.'

The nurse laughed, and I blushed again. What was I thinking, talking about climbing trees? They were looking for an auxiliary nurse, not a monkey.

'And you worked for Mr Sven Stolpe?' Dagmar said, looking again at the form.

'Yes.'

'*The* Sven Stolpe? The famous author?'

'Yes. I worked in his house in Malexander. Though, sometimes I went with him to Stockholm, which was very exciting.'

'Working with Sven Stolpe is certainly impressive,' she said.

She stood up and went to the window and looked out. She seemed even bigger now, out from behind the desk.

The sunlight made her look like a shadow against the window frame. I squinted, trying to make out her expression.

'And have you read his books?'

I didn't know whether to lie or not. I really wanted this

job. This could change my life. I was just a farm girl from Malexander.

'Yes,' I lied. I felt the palms of my hands sweat.

Dagmar turned. 'I like you, Kari, but you've never done anything like this before.'

She looked me up and down.

'A hospital is hard work. We deal with people's lives. Do you think you would be able for that pressure?' She stared at me, as if trying to read me.

'I like people,' I said. 'I want to be able to help.'

It sounded like something you should say. But this time it was the truth.

Dagmar nodded.

'Alright,' she said. 'I've made my decision.'

I sat up straighter in the chair.

'I'm willing to take a chance with you.'

'Thank you, Sister Dagmar. You won't regret this, I promise.'

'We'll see you on Monday, then. At seven o'clock. We'll give you a mentor and start training you straight away.'

Dagmar motioned to the nurse to hand her the notebook. She ripped a page out and scribbled something, and beckoned me to her.

'We will need certain documentation. This priest, Father Mats, lives nearby. He'll be able to help you with the forms we need. Tell him I sent you.'

And that was when I became an auxiliary nurse in Linköping, at the age of 17.

⸎

Linköping was not very far from the farm in Malexander, but it felt a world away.

Malexander was the kind of place where people talked about each other. A country village, where your business became everybody else's.

Our farm was like an oasis. Simon, Valborg and I had our world there. And it was beautiful. The countryside was an expanse of fields and lakes, and woodland that stretched as far as you could see. It was a happy place, but part of me always longed for the bright lights of Linköping. And so far, things were working out well. Better than well.

I was elated after the interview. But nervous too. It was a big opportunity. I hoped I would be a good nurse.

I went to see the priest, Father Mats, the same day as the interview, just as Dagmar had instructed. I knocked on his door.

'Come in!' a voice called.

His office was full of old books, piled high around a desk. I tried to make out where the voice had come from.

Father Mats appeared from behind the books. I explained that I needed documentation, proof of identity, for work.

'Sister Dagmar sent me.'

'I will do what I can. Sister Dagmar and I go back a long way.'

I gave him what little information I had. He jotted it down on the back of an envelope.

'Come back to me tomorrow,' he said.

When I went back the following day, he was busy fixing his collar and checking himself in the mirror.

'I'm on my way to a sermon, but I have your papers here.'

He handed them to me and apologised for not having time to stop and talk.

I opened the envelope and read the top of the document:

Name: Kari Andersson
Address: Malexander
Date of birth: 6 September 1944
Place of birth: Norway

'I'm sorry, but there's some mistake.'

'I don't think so,' he said, looking over the paper. 'This is what they gave me.'

'Who are "they"?'

'The people at the Department. It's all correct. I really have to go.' And then he was gone.

I stood there, staring at the form, at that word – 'Norway'. Surely it must be a mistake. I always thought I was Swedish. No one had ever mentioned Norway before. The next morning I handed the papers over to Dagmar, but I felt uneasy about it for the rest of the day.

I couldn't stop thinking about it. Later that week, I telephoned the Department of Immigration to find out why my papers said I was born in Norway.

'We can't help you,' said an official. Before I could say another word, they hung up.

I rang again the following day, and the day after that. Everyone I spoke to listened to my story, and then told me to speak to someone else. I must have tried a dozen times, and was about to give up when I was transferred again.

A woman came on the line.

'Yes, we have your details here. I think the information would have come from The Red Cross. If you came from abroad, your original file would have come through them. I'm afraid that's all we know. You'll have to stop calling here.'

Simon phoned later that evening. He asked me about work.

'It's good, Papa. Busy, but good. How is the farm?'

Hearing him talk, and imagining just where he was sitting, made me think of home.

'Simon ...' I was going to ask him about Norway, how it had appeared on this document as my birthplace.

'Yes, Kari?'

And then I stopped. I knew it made him uneasy when I asked about my past. I was adopted at the age of three, and all my life no one could tell me where I was born or who my biological parents were. What happened in those three years before I was adopted was a mystery. The 'three dark years', I called them. They were the gap in my life.

But where did Norway fit in? Is that where my real parents were? I wanted to ask him. But then I thought, why did I want to know, anyway? Simon and Valborg were my family. But on the other hand, I thought, didn't I have a right to know where I was from? All this was going through my mind.

'Kari, what is it? Is everything alright?'

'Oh, nothing, Papa. I'm just tired. That's all. A busy day at the hospital.'

And that was it. I decided not to ask. It would hurt him

too much. And I already knew the answer: 'I don't know.' The answer I had become accustomed to. I had tried time and time again to ask Simon about my early years. But it always seemed to make him sad when he couldn't give me the answers I needed. Or maybe he was sad because it reminded him that he wasn't there for the beginning of my life. That he wasn't my real father. Something he usually tried to forget.

I tried to put it out of my mind. I needed to conserve my energy. Work at the hospital was the toughest I had ever done. The hours were long and it was around the clock, but I loved it. It gave me a purpose. I had to learn quickly about medicine and how hospitals worked. And with the new job, I built a new life.

I moved into an apartment with a girl named Yvonne and I started to make good friends at work.

In a short space of time, my life changed beyond recognition. I now had a home of my own, something I had always wanted.

The apartment was small, and maybe a little shabby, but it was mine. It felt like my own space.

I will never forget taking the key and putting it in the lock for the first time. I was growing up.

I promised myself to think only about the future and not to get hung up about the past. I decided to leave it behind me, where it belonged.

I went to dancehalls and cafés in and around Linköping. The freedom was exhilarating. It was everything I imagined it would be.

I worked hard, and enjoyed life in the city, and with

each year that passed, Linköping felt more and more like home.

But the past has a way of catching up with you, no matter how much you look to the future. Four years later, in 1965, it did just that.

I was 21 years old that year. Up to then, everything was normal – or, at least, I thought it was normal. But 1965 was a watershed year. When I look back, I think of everything that happened after that as happening to a different person, a different Kari.

That is why I remember that night so well. The night that changed everything.

It was late. I had finished my shift in the hospital and was making my way through the deserted streets of Linköping, with nothing to light my way but the dim glow of street lamps. There was an eerie atmosphere about that particular night. I felt like something was ready to leap out at me from the shadows.

The last block felt the longest. Some of the lamps were flickering on and off like fireflies. But at least I could see my apartment building now.

I could feel the draw of indoors, and the safety of my bed after the long shift on the hospital ward.

And then with home in sight, I heard a piercing screech from behind. I jumped. My heart raced. In my peripheral vision, I saw a cat scurry down a side street, pursued by another cat. I felt relief – for myself, not for the pursued cat – and quickened my pace, thinking how cruel nature can be in its urge to reproduce itself. Cats might have nine lives, but some of those must be full of pain.

Working in the hospital made me familiar with pain. I saw it every day, and rather than become inured, I seemed to become more sensitive to it with each passing year.

I opened the door into the apartment block and made my way up the stairs to my own front door. Home.

It was a relief to be inside, safe from the world.

I kicked off my shoes and settled into the armchair by the window, and closed my eyes. I tried to let the tensions of the hospital lift. Sleep would come soon, but not yet.

I hadn't eaten all day. I tried to remember what food I had in the cupboard, or if there was any. I usually tried to eat well, but it was difficult when I was working odd hours. Whenever I went back to the farm, Valborg nagged me to watch my diet. Knowing how difficult it was for me to manage on my own, she and Simon spoiled me with home-cooked meals when I visited.

As I sat by the window that night in my city apartment, I could almost taste the spicy meatballs of the farm and feel the warmth of the Malexander kitchen fire on my legs. It seemed perfect, until I imagined Valborg's voice, scolding me as she spotted the torn hem of my tunic, and the loose white threads. Valborg, who was always mothering me, no matter how old I became.

'How do you go to work like that? Have you no pride in your nurse's uniform?'

I had snagged my tunic on one of the hospital beds the previous week and hadn't got round to mending it. That would never pass Valborg's eagle eye.

I smiled at the thoughts of her. She meant well. My mother, in every way but one.

There was a noise coming from under the window. I leaned forward and looked out. I could see a couple squabbling in the street below.

I tried to make out what they were saying. I held my breath so I could listen with my whole body.

Working the late shift could be lonely, so when I came home, I loved watching strangers and their lives from the window of my room. I loved imagining where they went to dinner, and where they called home.

I watched this couple, who now seemed to have made up. They kissed and then walked back down the street in the direction I had come. I wondered what it would be like to be like them, to be in love. The street didn't seem eerie any more.

My mind was too full of the happenings of the day to sleep. It was like I had to unwind the coil of the day before I could start the night.

That day had begun like any other. We were busy at the hospital, as always. Mrs Petersen had been in for blood tests again and she had been admitted. She was a regular patient who had taken a shine to me over the years.

'Call me Katherine. People only call me Mrs Petersen when they're giving me bills!' she'd say. She had a good sense of humour. We knew how to make each other laugh.

I rolled her into the ward in her wheelchair. The wheels squeaked as they turned on the polished floor. I took the blanket from her lap and lifted her into the bed. Her old bones were as light as a bird's.

She sat up in the bed.

'Kari, where did they find you?' she said, placing her hand on my arm.

'I wish I knew,' I said.

'Your parents must be very proud of you. You've been like a daughter to me these last few months. Tell your mother that. Tell her she is lucky to have a daughter like you.'

I liked Katherine Petersen. I liked all of my patients.

The hours passed quickly. Before I knew it, it was 11 o'clock. Time for coffee and a break.

The nurses' room was full of excitement when I got there. I wondered what all the chatter was about. Then I saw a huge bunch of roses tied with a red ribbon in the middle of the table, and a card that read 'Sofia'.

'Wow!' said Nina, a trainee nurse from Stockholm. 'Who are those lovely flowers for?'

'Not me,' I said. 'Sofia. See the card.'

Sofia came in just then.

'For me?'

She picked up the flowers like she was about to dance with them. The other nurses cheered and Sofia blushed.

She told us she was introducing her boyfriend to her parents that night for the first time. Her mother and father were driving up from the country.

'My mother's even baking a cake for tonight,' she said. 'She must have high hopes. She only makes the effort when she thinks they sound good. I can't wait for him to meet her. He'll finally be able to put a face to all the stories. And my mother, she looks just like me. I hope that doesn't put him off.'

She laughed and tilted her head as she said it, and I could almost imagine her mother.

For the rest of the shift, I kept thinking of Sofia, as she stood by the window, the light catching her blonde hair. I didn't look at all like my mother, like Valborg. Or like Simon either. In fact, I didn't know a single person in the world who looked just like me.

I couldn't help imagining what it would be like if I brought a boyfriend back to the farm to meet Simon and Valborg. I knew they would be happy for me. Of course they would.

I tried to imagine how it would go. I could see them making a fuss of us as we pulled up into the farmyard. Simon would come up from the fields to greet us, waving as he made his way towards the house, our country cottage by the stream.

He would stumble over the stony Malexander ground, excited to see me coming. He would give me a hug – he was great for hugs – and we'd make our way inside to the familiar smell of home cooking, and the warmth of the kitchen.

Valborg would have all the food laid out, a smörgåsbord of her special treats – freshly baked bread, pea soup, smoked herring and cream cakes. In my mind, I could see her stoking the open fire. When she saw us coming she'd turn to examine the newcomer, eyeing my boyfriend, checking for signs that he thought the cottage too modest. She was house-proud by nature, and made a lot of the little she had. When she was satisfied he wasn't looking down on her, she would extend a hand to greet him.

We would laugh and talk. I would give him a tour. I would take him up into my old room, with a bed just big enough for one, and show him the crocheted tablecloth that I had worked on all summer when I was a young girl, sitting by the wooden table Simon had carved especially for me.

Through the window, overlooking the fields, I would show him where we kept our cows and pigs. I would point in the direction of the school, just up the road, and take him through the story of my life in Malexander, so that he would really understand who I was.

It would all be fine as long as he didn't ask too many questions. And then we would go back downstairs and drink coffee, all of us sitting around the table.

As I imagined the scene, a sadness came over me. Simon and Valborg had given me so much, but there was something I could never give them.

Any children I would bear in the future would not be their *real* grandchildren. They wouldn't look like them or have their genes. I could never give them that. I wasn't family. Not really. I wasn't blood. And if I wasn't that, what was I?

∽⚭∽

As I looked out the window of my apartment that night, in the spring of 1965, the word 'Norway' came into my mind again. I had tried to forget about it, but every time I passed Dagmar's filing cabinet I knew that sheet of paper was there, and that word 'Norway' was written on it.

Sweden was the only home I had ever known. I thought of Mrs Petersen, about what she said. I was like a daughter to her. What if one day my real mother walked into the hospital where I worked, and I passed her by without a word? Not knowing.

Over the years, I had often thought about trying to find out who my real mother was. Now that I was away from the farm, the feeling was even stronger. At night time especially it came, and it would sometimes stop me from sleeping.

That night, I was thinking of Sofia's flowers, and her mother, and the way her life just seemed to make sense. I was happy for her. But I wanted all those things too. I didn't know who my real mother and father were. I sat there in the apartment for a long time, feeling alone, and looking out into the dark and empty street. It was looking eerie again.

Then, on an impulse, I made the decision. I went to the bureau in the corner of the room, grabbed a pen and paper and began writing. The pen hardly left the page until the deed was done.

I sealed the envelope and wrote in bold letters across the front, 'THE RED CROSS'. I decided this would be my final attempt to find my real parents. If this came to nothing, I would simply leave the past alone.

I realised, then, that I didn't know the address. The weight of that realisation was almost paralysing. I don't know why, but I feared that if I didn't get my letter to The Red Cross that very night, all would be lost.

I thumbed through the phone book, my index finger

searching the pages. R... Re... Red Cross – there it was, with the address in Stockholm.

I addressed the envelope and stamped it. My hand was shaking. I felt guilty now. Like I was betraying Simon. Valborg would be pragmatic, that was her way. But Simon would feel it. He would accuse me with his eyes.

That night, I could only think about myself. I grabbed my coat and headed back out. I was halfway down the street when I realised I'd forgotten my gloves. But I didn't care. My right hand clenched the envelope, in case anyone dared stop me.

All my life I had felt that the longer I waited, the less chance I would have of discovering my true identity. And I had let it go, many times, but it was always there. And lately, for some reason, I felt time was running out. As every day slipped by, I worried they were slipping away. My real parents. Now, at last I was doing something. I was reaching out, trying to grab hold of them before it was too late.

I wasn't sure where I was going. I remembered seeing a postbox in the main square, which was at least 15 minutes' walk away. I was almost running. A drunk man leaning against a wall called out to me.

'Some night to be on your own. I'll keep you warm, love.'

I walked even faster. I could feel his eyes on me. I could hear a bottle in his hand clink against the wall.

At last I turned a corner and saw the clock in the middle of the square. Its hands were drawing closer together, towards midnight. My eyes surveyed the empty square, frantically searching for the postbox. Had I imagined it? And then I saw it, near an old antique shop.

I opened the metal flap. It seemed to bite my hand as I pushed the letter through, but I held its jaw open and listened as my letter fluttered down into the tray. I let the flap slap shut. I felt like my life hung in the balance between that tray and the destination of the letter. And I thought again of what Simon would feel. But I also imagined, for the second time that day, that look they might have if I brought someone home to meet them – that look that said I wasn't their own. And my eyes filled with tears.

I had made my decision, and there was no going back. Whatever happened after that moment was of my making. I knew that. And I felt the only way I could have an honest future for myself was to fill the gaps in my past. It seemed to me such a fundamental thing – to know who I was. I had to at least try. Even if I never heard back, at least I would know I had done everything I could.

I could feel all this, deep down, and yet, standing there in that empty square, I felt colder all of a sudden, exposed, without the security of my envelope. I felt suddenly tiny, a woman without a past, or present, or future. And then, as if to mock me, the clock struck midnight.

3

A chance encounter

I remember a lot of things about that night in 1965, but I can't remember getting home after posting that letter to The Red Cross. The next day, I woke up around noon. I was late for work – very late. I felt as if I had been drinking, with only vague recollections of the night before. My head was pounding. It all felt like I had dreamed it.

Even though I was late for work, I took a long, hot shower. I let the water flow over my pounding head, and stood there for some time, naked and tired, wondering how I could face the day ahead.

As I was leaving the apartment, I caught a glimpse of myself in the hall mirror. There were dark circles under my eyes. My tunic was still torn, and my hair was a mess. I didn't look like myself. I was usually so well put together – careful to be clean and tidy. What was happening to me recently? I thought about the letter I had written the night before. I wondered if I had done the right thing. But looking at my reflection, the words came to my mind again: 'Who am I?' I was kind, I suppose. People told me

that. I think I got that from Simon. But there were some things that were part of me that couldn't have come from him or Valborg. Some things are genetic. My shape, for instance. I was slim, but sturdy too. I had always been a strong girl. Self-assured. But what made me this way? Were my parents like this? Were they kind? Could they be impatient sometimes? Or a little awkward? I was a tomboy when I was younger. But I had been a beautiful child. Where did I get that from? Did my mother or father have the same soft blue eyes, the same fair hair? Did they laugh a lot? Were they in love? My mind was full of questions. The same questions I had wondered all my life. But they seemed more pressing now, all of a sudden. Maybe because I was out on my own trying to reinvent myself, to find out who I was. Like all young people do when they leave home.

But there was work to do. I had to go. I ran my fingers through my hair. I had started wearing it shorter. It was easier to manage. It made me feel a bit older too, a bit more professional. I tried to tidy myself as best I could until I looked presentable. I took a deep breath. Normal life had to continue. I decided that yes, I had done the right thing. If my biological parents were out there I needed to know who they were, in order to finally know who I was. I picked up my handbag, put on my coat and walked to work. It gave me time to think.

The hospital was busy that day, as all days, but I got through it. It was busy all week and I got through that too. I have always been good at getting on with things. I think it comes from farm life. If it's broken, you fix it.

If it's needed, you fetch it. It was the way I was raised. I was glad of work to do. It helped to distract me from thoughts of where my letter was and what was being done, if anything. I was working longer hours, and it felt like I was going home only to go to sleep, get up and go back to work again.

I was on my way home one wet evening when I realised I had forgotten to get groceries – again. It was late. Everything was closed, so I decided I would treat myself to dinner in my favourite restaurant around the corner from the apartment.

It was a plain restaurant, but I liked it. I used to go there a lot when I first moved to Linköping, before I got into a routine, when I was new to living away from home.

There was a soft glow from inside, and as you entered, a bell at the top of the door gave a friendly 'ding' to let them know you were there. The waiters knew me, and were always welcoming.

The place was famous for its pastries. They were said to serve the best apple strudel in all of Sweden – maybe the world.

I joined the queue and chose the soup. The restaurant was crowded, mostly with young people. More so even than usual. There must have been a student event on in the local hall.

I felt a little out of place that night, my nurse's tunic sticking out from under my coat. I tried to find an empty table, but they were all taken.

I heard a man's voice. 'There's a seat over here.'

He was at the opposite end of the room. He was half

standing, and waving to get my attention. I took one last frantic look around, hoping another seat would materialise so I could decline his invitation, but none did, and so I went, carrying my bowl of chicken soup, to sit across from this stranger.

'Thank you,' I said as I sat down. I placed my bowl and cutlery on the table, in a way that implied distance and separateness: a division of the table, rather than a sharing of it.

I took off my coat and scarf. I was aware the man's eyes were on me. I smiled at him, and for the first time, made eye contact. He was handsome. He had blue eyes and dark brown hair.

I felt self-conscious. I took a spoonful of soup. It was scalding. I wanted to spit it out, but instead, swallowed and braced myself for the searing heat that made its way slowly down my throat. I hoped he hadn't noticed.

'Hot?' he said, smiling.

'Just a little.' I felt so awkward.

I continued to eat my soup, as he read a newspaper and sipped his coffee. We were pretending to be in our own worlds, but there was an energy there.

I was nervous and couldn't think of anything to say. He had been staring at the same paragraph since I sat down. A group of students at the next table were arguing about Prime Minister Erlander and the Social Democratic Party.

'He'll never last the year!'

'Of course he will. The party is still the most popular in the country!'

'What does that say about the country!' The debate

was heated, and they spoke loudly over the noise of the restaurant, making our silence seem even more pronounced.

'Have you tried the apple strudel?' I asked, just for something to say, and immediately regretted it. Of all the things I could have said, I had chosen to talk about the strudel.

The next few seconds felt like an eternity, and then to my relief he said, 'Actually, I have heard about this famous apple strudel. But I haven't been fortunate enough to try it yet.'

At that moment, Gilles came by to take my empty bowl. He always looked a little out of breath and run off his feet. He produced a notebook and pen from his apron.

'Can I get the lovely couple some dessert?'

I could feel myself blushing. Gilles! He knew what he was doing. He was always teasing me for being alone.

'I think it'll have to be the apple strudel,' said my table friend, looking over at me.

'Why not?' I said.

'Daniel,' he said, putting out his hand. 'I think we should know each other's names if we're going to share a dessert.' He had a cheeky smile.

'Kari.'

'Nice to meet you, Kari.'

He looked at me. 'So how's work at the hospital?'

'What? How did you ...?' I'd forgotten I was wearing my uniform.

I laughed. 'Oh, of course ...'

We talked for what must have been more than hour

over our strudel, neither of us wanting to take the last bite, each trying to prolong the conversation. I didn't even notice that all the students had left. The restaurant was quiet, and Gilles was packing up for the night.

Daniel was a mathematician. I tried not to look too impressed when he told me this. I was never good at numbers. I count on my fingers. My only experience of mathematics was in school in Malexander, and involved exercise books full of corrections in red ink. Gilles cleared his throat as he wiped down the serving counter, and I could tell it was time to leave.

Daniel helped me with my coat, and seemed a perfect gentleman. When we got outside he insisted on walking me home. He lived in the opposite direction, but said it was too late for me to walk alone. I didn't tell him that I walked this way every evening on my own. I was glad of his company.

When we arrived at the door of my apartment building we were unsure how to end the evening. It always seemed so smooth in the movies. I thought of Audrey Hepburn at the crucial moment when Humphrey Bogart leans in, their lips meet and the music builds to confirm that yes, indeed, this night was a success. Standing there, under the street lamps, especially the flickering one, I suddenly felt very nervous. We had talked effortlessly the whole way home, but now, the air felt tense. We were both silent for a moment. I looked down at my feet, waiting for him to make the next move, and then a loud noise came from the laneway. The cats again, clawing at one another. And the spell was broken. This was not to be a movie moment.

Daniel could sense my disappointment. 'Can I bring you for coffee, Kari?' he asked.

'Yes, I'd love that.'

'Ok, I'll see you on Saturday. I'll call here around noon, if that suits.' I nodded and he walked away, smiling.

I couldn't wait to run upstairs to tell Yvonne everything about my evening with this handsome stranger.

When I got to my door on the third floor, I felt strange, and wondered if it was possible to miss someone you had just met.

Inside there was a pile of letters on the floor. As usual, the first thing I did was check them. All bills. It had been weeks now since I had written to The Red Cross.

I threw the envelopes back in the corner of the hall, determined not to let anything get me down, not that night.

Yvonne was already asleep. I lay in bed, replaying every moment of the evening, reliving the conversations until I drifted off to sleep.

∽✌∼

Daniel and I went for coffee that Saturday in a café overlooking the Stångån river. I loved being by the river. It reminded me of the stream that ran through the farm in Malexander. We sipped our coffees and talked and talked – about books, and music, and about our childhoods, and where we grew up.

I could see his interest peak when I mentioned having worked for Sven Stolpe. I was getting a lot of mileage out of my connection to this famous author.

I told Daniel how it was that I had come to work as Sven Stolpe's helper when I was a young girl. I told him about the big yellow house two kilometres from my home in Malexander. How I would walk there every day after school whether it was sunny or snowing.

I told him how, before the author ever came to live there, Simon had got me a job at this house through a friend of his, to work as a housekeeper. About how I showed up on the first day for work to find that the sole occupant of the house was a widow. Her husband, a successful businessman, had died of a heart attack. Her children were all grown up and had moved away. Her face was pale, and she wore black every day, in a constant state of mourning.

She was cold, as if she carried sorrow with her into every room in that big house. She spent all day indoors. I would clean the rooms, dust cobwebs from the ceilings, and wipe down the windows.

And then came my favourite part of the day – the gardening. I always preferred to be outdoors. Especially when I was at that house. The bright colours of the garden lifted my spirits, taking me away from the gloom of the house, if only for an hour or two.

In the evening I would cook for the widow and serve her dinner as she sat alone, at the head of a long mahogany dining table. I wondered how a life gets to be that way. What has to happen in life to leave you sitting alone, rich, and sad. And she was that, deeply sad.

But part of it was her own choosing. I would have kept her company, if she had let me. But any time I tried to talk to her it seemed to make her uncomfortable. She gave one-word answers, and thought of other chores I had to do, which would take me out of the room. She insisted I ate on my own in the servants' quarters. So we were both alone, sitting in separate rooms, listening to the creaking of the house as the wind howled through the chimneys.

The first day I went to work for her, I was frightened by her silence. I came home and told Simon and Valborg I was never going back. Simon sat me down and told me that I had to go back, and I had to keep working for her for the rest of the week. If at the end of the week I still felt the same, then I could quit, but he said I had to give everything a reasonable try. It was one of his many lessons.

I stayed for a week, and the week turned into a month, and before I knew it I had been there a year. I had seen the flowers I planted bloom.

I felt sorry for the widow. I felt protective of her, even though I was very young. If I didn't come, then no one would for days, maybe weeks, on end. So I kept coming, in case one day she needed help and nobody was there. I think she appreciated it, in her own way. She never said it though. She never asked me about myself either. I still ate on my own, and she made me wear a uniform – a white apron. She insisted that it always be starched and clean. She was very particular about that. Maybe it was to keep me in my place, I don't know.

One day, she came back from a trip to the village, and told me to go to the bathroom and make myself presentable. She looked down at my apron, inspecting it for stains.

'Tidy yourself, and wait in the study.'

I went to the study and waited.

A few minutes later a tall, middle-aged man came through the door. He was wearing a suit with a folded handkerchief in his lapel. He had a side parting in his hair and a pair of dark, thick-rimmed glasses perched on his nose. He was like no one I had ever seen in Malexander. He took a moment to examine the room, and then to examine me.

'Alright,' he said, and left. Later, the widow told me that she was selling the house, and that this man, Sven Stolpe, was going to buy it.

Things moved quickly. The widow packed up her life in a few small boxes. Her children came back to squabble over the antique furniture and old paintings, the things she wasn't taking with her. And then, they were gone again. The house was empty. And a week later, Sven Stolpe moved in.

He had a young family of four children, including a girl about my own age. Her name was Lisette. There was life in the house again. He filled the old bookcases with leather-bound books that had different-colour spines.

He took me aside the first day I came to the house after he had moved in. I thought he was going to tell me I wasn't needed anymore. Instead, he told me to call him Sven. He asked me my name, and where I came from and about my school. And then he said, 'Kari, I can see you're smart.' It was the first time anyone had ever said anything like that to me.

'I don't want you to be our cleaner, Kari, we can cook

and clean for ourselves, but I do need a helper. Can you do that?'

He was writing a book about Queen Christina of Sweden. I didn't know anything about her. I knew Gustaf VI was King, but I knew nothing of the kings and queens who had come before him. I nodded in agreement anyway. I was very excited by this man. I wanted him to like me. There was one condition though.

'No apron!' he said.

My uniform was decommissioned there and then.

From then on, I could come and go as I pleased. My job was to help him find the books he needed in his library, and to help him organise his notes. It was hard at first, but I wanted to do well for him, so I learned fast. I ate with the rest of the family, and loved being around Sven Stolpe. He was unlike anyone I had ever met. He played the piano loudly and badly. He sang as he banged the keys. I think it helped him to think. And when ideas came to him, he worried they would disappear just as quickly as they came. He was like a butterfly catcher with a hole in his net. He would jump up and run to his study to write the idea down. It happened in the middle of a sentence sometimes, or between mouthfuls at the dinner table.

I enjoyed the journeys most of all. As a small child, I had often dreamed that I was flying. I would get higher and higher, until I was soaring over Malexander, above the clouds. I could fly anywhere in my dreams. I imagined what the rest of the world looked like, because I had never known anything other than Malexander. Until I met the Stolpes. They opened up another world for me. Sven

Stolpe told us stories about all the wonderful places he had been.

As they got to know me better, they started to take me with them on their trips to the city. The whole family would go to Stockholm and I would go with them. We would pile into the car and head off. I had never known such excitement.

Sven and his wife Karin were often invited to big award ceremonies, and sometimes Lisette and I would go with them. I remembered one trip in particular. We were going to meet a group of famous actors for dinner. We arrived in Stockholm and put on our best dresses.

But when we reached the restaurant where the ceremony was taking place, the actors were very drunk. They laughed and joked across the table, and had no interest in talking to us. They thought us too young to join in their conversation. Karin looked embarrassed by the actors' behaviour and insisted on bringing us home early, back to the Stolpes' city apartment. In the safety of the apartment, Lisette and I jumped into the four-poster bed together, and huddled under the sheets, staying up all night, telling ghost stories. That was the best part of all.

‍✤‍

Daniel loved hearing about Sven Stolpe. He read a lot and was fascinated by the world of authors. No one ever knew why Sven Stolpe moved to sleepy Malexander. It was a beautiful place, but there was nothing there, only land and farmers to till it. But I was glad he had moved there and that I was like a daughter to him. He opened up my world. I remember the day a reporter from a magazine came to the house. She asked Sven Stolpe how many children he had. He nodded to me as I put the tea down beside him and said, 'Here's one of them!'

'Sven Stolpe showed me a different life. I think he gave me the courage to leave Malexander,' I said to Daniel.

'He sounds like an incredible man,' Daniel said. 'You seem to have been really taken by him.'

I felt embarrassed when I looked down at our empty coffee cups, and realised I had been talking non-stop for half an hour. Everything seemed to spill out of me when I was around Daniel. But he didn't seem to mind.

Our first official date had gone well. That same week he invited me to dinner, then to the theatre. We were getting to know each other, and there was an energy he brought with him that I couldn't seem to get enough of. I never knew what he was going to do next. He was unpredictable, spontaneous – everything I wasn't. But he brought out the mischief in me. We laughed a lot when we were together. And we could be serious too.

One evening we were sitting in the living room sharing a bottle of wine. Daniel was pacing about the room, telling me his theory about the number of soldiers Hitler had in the war, and how that affected his chances against the Allies. He believed history and mathematics were linked.

'In order to understand one, we must master the other.'

I was never interested in history.

He spoke so quickly, like he couldn't stop the thoughts from coming, he was so passionate. I loved hearing him talk like that. In fact everybody loved him. Sometimes I wondered what he saw in me. Why he chose me above all the others. I felt so lucky to be with him. I watched him pacing while I lay back in my chair, drinking a glass of wine. Then the key turned in the lock, and Yvonne came in.

'Kari – post for you,' she said, throwing some letters on the hall table as she made her way towards the kitchen.

My heart still fluttered every time there was post. I just kept thinking, what if this is it? I felt like I was constantly waiting for something to happen. I tried to control it. I assumed unopened envelopes were bills, but a little part of me wondered every time something came through the letterbox if it might be a reply to my letter to The Red Cross. I opened the envelopes carefully – one was a letter from the hospital, and the other was from a friend who had moved to Stockholm six months earlier. I couldn't hide my disappointment.

Daniel had stopped talking. He was studying me. I always felt a bit uneasy when he didn't talk. Even his silence was loaded with energy. He cleared his throat, and I could tell he wanted to ask me something.

'What are you hoping for?'

'What?'

'What are you hoping for?' he repeated, putting emphasis on *hoping,* like it would make the question clearer.

'Well … I'm hoping that Dagmar will come in to work tomorrow and tell me to take the rest of the week off. That and world peace. Yes, that would be good too. That's what I'm hoping for.'

'Very funny. You know what I mean. I've seen you, every time a letter comes through the door. You almost jump out of your skin. What is it?'

'It's nothing.' I looked out the window, wishing he'd stop trying to figure me out.

'It's late,' I said. 'I think you should go. I have to be up early.'

We didn't bring it up again, and as the weeks went by, I paid more attention to Daniel and less to the post coming through the door, until eventually I forgot about it entirely.

Summer came. It was warm, and the days were long. Linköping was looking its best. Things were going well with Daniel, and I decided to host a party – our first.

The flat was small, so we were all a little cramped, but it was nice. I loved having everyone together.

Sofia brought her boyfriend Carl. He was everything she had said he was. When I saw him I thought of the bunch of roses in the nurses' room that day, with the big red ribbon. And it reminded me of the day I decided to write to The Red Cross. It felt like a long time ago now. I smiled and shook his hand as Sofia introduced us. And I remembered my other decision that day – I vowed that this would be my final attempt to find my real parents, and if this failed, I would stop looking.

So that's what I would do, I thought. Stop looking. Besides, things were different now. I had Daniel. I felt relieved all of a sudden, like that decision had already come into play. I wouldn't want anymore, I'd accept. I felt ready to enjoy the company of people around me – real people who existed right there in front of me.

Carl was lovely. He made his way around the room, getting to know everyone. But it was Daniel who stole the show that night. He started the first verse of Evert Taube's song *Brevet Från Lillan*, and everyone joined in. We sang Swedish songs, and laughed and danced until daylight. I looked over at Daniel playing the guitar and I found myself quiet, still, just staring at him and smiling.

'I love you,' I said later, when everyone was gone. I had never felt so afraid as when I said those three words.

Daniel looked at me and said, 'I love you too.'

If I was given a wish then, it would have been that we could stay that way forever, there in that moment, in my apartment in Linköping.

I was exhausted the next day in work, and to make matters worse, Dagmar had asked me to do a double shift. By the time I got to the hospital she was on the warpath. She was marching through the corridors, yelling instructions at the nurses. My stomach churned. It was going to be one of *those* days. I threw my coat on the back of a chair, thinking I'd managed to sneak in unnoticed.

'You're late!' Dagmar yelled, and gave me a long list of things to do. They had closed down one of the units, and laid off some of the nurses, so we were all working overtime to keep the hospital going.

I decided to go for a quick sleep during my few hours off, between shifts. I made my way to the small bedroom off the nurses' room. It was like a utility closet, just big enough for two small bunk beds. I hung my uniform on the metal rail of the bed and slipped under the sheets on the bottom bunk, and closed my eyes. It wasn't long before I was in a deep sleep. I had three hours before my next shift, and I wanted to make the most of them.

I don't know how long I had been asleep when I awoke to the feeling of someone's hot breath against my face. I was disorientated. I felt a hand slide up my thigh, and heavy breathing in my ear.

I was suddenly wide awake. I shot up, pushed the hand away from me, and kicked out with my legs. My attacker fell to the floor. I pulled the sheets around me. In the darkness I could make out a woman's face. I recognised her. She worked in the hospital. I froze in fear. She scrambled up from the floor and left the room.

I was left there in the darkness in shock. I stayed like that for what felt like the longest time, staring at the bunk above me. I didn't want to leave the room in case she was there. I imagined her breathing against the door outside, leering, waiting for me.

I felt angry and confused. And most of all I felt exhausted. I wanted so badly to go back to sleep, but I couldn't close my eyes for fear she would return.

I had to go back to work though. Dagmar would be looking for me. I fastened my bra and put my uniform back on. I took a deep breath, gathered myself, and left the room. I tried to behave as though nothing had happened.

I kept to myself for the rest of the day. But that evening, when I walked into one of the wards, there she was, that woman.

She whispered in my ear, with that same hot breath against my face, 'No one will believe you.'

She gave me a threatening look and walked out. My

hands were shaking. I gathered a bundle of patients' files from the nurses' station, but as I turned to leave, I lost my grip, and the papers fell to the floor. As I bent down to pick them up I could feel the tears welling, and a lump forming in my throat.

That night Daniel was waiting outside the hospital to walk me home. We were going to eat in the restaurant around the corner, the one where we first met. He could tell there was something wrong with me.

'What's happened, Kari? You're white as a ghost.'

I burst into tears and told him everything. He was angry. I had never seen him like that before.

'She did *what*? You have to tell the authorities, Kari. You have to tell someone.'

I knew that I couldn't tell anyone, and I felt angry at him for saying I should.

'Let's just forget about this place. In fact, let's go away from here tonight. Go to a different city. You should never have to work here again.'

I wished he would just listen. That he wouldn't try to solve everything all at once. He was too full of energy for me that night. He wanted to leave everything, just disappear.

'This isn't helping, Daniel. Have you any idea how impractical that is?'

'Well, what then? You can't just do nothing.'

'I'm not doing nothing, Daniel. I'm just upset.'

'Why don't you go back to Malexander, then? Just for a little while even.'

'You think I can't cope here? I've always coped. Long before I met you.'

'You're not used to the city, Kari. You're different.'

And in that moment, maybe because of what had happened earlier, I felt a rage in me. Before I knew what I was doing, I grabbed his satchel of books, and, without thinking, threw them into the river.

I turned and ran down the street. I didn't look back to see his reaction. I just kept running until I reached home.

4

The call

The next day I waited to hear from Daniel. Nothing. Nor the day after that. Four days went by and I still hadn't heard from him. I wondered if he would ever forgive me.

And when I thought it over, I realised he was just trying to help. And maybe he was right after all. Maybe it would be good to take some time off. I was back in work, but I didn't feel myself. By the time the weekend came, and still no word from Daniel, I decided I would go back to the farm in Malexander. Just for a few days' rest.

It was good to be back there. I helped Simon to milk the cows and we joked about the old days, when I used to follow him around the farm like a puppy. And how I would sometimes spend afternoons with my grandmother, Simon's mother. Her name was Anna. She was a kind, gentle woman and I loved visiting her as a child. I would help her water the flowers in her garden, and she would tell me stories about Simon when he was young.

She had long, grey hair, which she wore in a bun. When we were talking, she would take the clip out and sigh, and allow her hair roll down to her waist. I was the only one who knew what she looked like with her hair down. It was our secret. Like we were in a fairytale. When anyone else came to visit, she pinned her hair up again.

She lived in a neighbourhood with lots of other old people. I felt like they were all my grandparents. They always seemed glad to see me coming.

'Kari, you've grown so big!' they would say. Or, 'Give me a hug, Kari!'

One day when I was about seven, a new man came to live on my grandmother's street. He was in the house that a lady called Mrs Ekland used to be in before the priest came to visit and we never saw her again. The old man asked me where I was from.

'I'm from here, from Malexander,' I said.

I heard some of the old women whispering, as if they knew something about me. It made me feel strange.

I asked my grandmother if it was not true that I was from Malexander. She changed the subject and gave me a treat.

'None of that matters. Kari, you're my best girl. Here, take this,' and she gave me a big wedge of chocolate cake.

But the way she looked at me told me there was more to it than she would say. That look stayed with me. Whenever I felt uncomfortable in the world afterwards, I would remember that look, and I would feel like I was out of the frame somehow, out of the picture. Like a jigsaw piece that couldn't fit in.

And then Simon came to collect me as he always did, on the bicycle, and we cycled back home through the fields, and I asked him about the stories I had heard about him, of when he was young. He always laughed.

'Don't believe everything your grandmother tells you!'

But he seemed to remember a lot on the days we visited his mother.

'See that bridge over there? That's where I kissed my first girlfriend, when I was just ten years old.'

I laughed at the thought of it.

'And that field over there … That's where I scored my first goal. I used to play football there after school.'

And then he would reach over and tickle me, and make me howl with laughter, as I held on tight to the bar of the bicycle. Those were memorable days. It was our time, and I treasured every minute.

I loved Malexander, but one day Simon told me to leave. He knew there was more for me in the world. I think he believed country life didn't have a lot to offer a young girl growing up. His own life was not ideal.

He and Valborg didn't have much to say to one another. She did the things that a wife should do, but I never saw them laugh together when they were alone, or share any kind of intimacy. They just performed their roles. She cooked, he worked the land, and so it went on, day after day. I knew all this. I knew he wanted more for me. So I left. But even though I had moved away, I still missed the farm. And being there made me realise how much I missed it.

The days passed all too quickly in Malexander, and soon it was time to go back to Linköping. Valborg gave me pies she had baked, and I was looking forward to eating them during the week, after work, famished after my hospital shift.

Driving back, I kept the windows of the car down, trying to take it all in, enjoying the country smells. But as I approached the city, the streets felt like my streets. It was strange to think that in a few short years my life had changed so quickly, and so much.

∽≫∽

The next morning I woke to the sound of the telephone ringing.

I picked up the phone.

It was a woman's voice. 'This is Freida Eriksson,' she said.

I didn't know anyone by that name. I was disappointed it wasn't Daniel.

'I'm sorry. I think you have the wrong number.' I was about to hang up.

'Is this Kari Andersson?'

'Yes,' I said. 'What is this about?'

'I have some information for you. I have the answer to your question. The question in your letter.'

I could hardly breathe.

'Hello … are you there?'

'Yes. I'm here.'

I was barely able to get the words out. It was possible that this woman knew more about me than I did. Part of me wanted to hang up the phone.

'I know who your mother is.'

I couldn't speak now even if I knew what to say.

'I know this will come as a shock to you.' She paused for a moment, and all I could hear was the faint crackle of the telephone line.

'You have a Norwegian mother, and a German father.'

I said nothing.

'Kari?' she said. 'Are you there? Are you alright?'

'Yes,' I said. I didn't know which question I was answering.

'I have located your mother. She is alive. She is living in Oslo.'

The woman paused, and then her tone changed.

'I ... I think *she* should tell you about your father ... It's not my place.'

'What? Why can't you tell me? What do you mean it's not your place? Who is my father?'

'I'm afraid I'm not authorised ...'

'Authorised by whom?' I felt confused, shocked. I didn't know what to think.

I couldn't understand what all the mystery was about. Why couldn't she tell me about my father? I started to think that this might be some kind of joke. Someone who had found the letter. She said she was from The Red Cross, but I didn't even know if I had addressed the letter correctly.

'I have arranged everything,' she said, her tone more officious. It was starting to feel real.

'Your tickets have been bought for you. You travel tomorrow. You just have to go to the train station and collect them. And there will be a letter there too, with your mother's home address. Kari? Kari, are you there?'

I let the receiver fall to the floor.

I could hear her voice as if she was calling to me from a distance, from somewhere out there in the city, many blocks away.

'Kari? Kari? Are you there?'

I walked back to the bedroom and climbed into bed and pulled the blankets over me. Why wouldn't she tell me about my father? I lay there for what felt like hours, trying to piece it all together. She was alive. My mother was alive.

I wondered if Valborg and Simon knew who my parents were all along. Valborg hadn't been able to have children. I even wondered if maybe they had stolen me from my real parents. Maybe that's why they never told me anything about my past. They didn't want me to find out. And then I felt guilty for thinking that. My head hurt. I pressed my face down into the pillow.

I decided not to go to work. I disconnected the phone. I didn't want any more calls. And then I thought, what if I've broken the line, and that woman can't call again? I plugged it back in, picked up the receiver and heard the dial tone.

I lay on the bed. I tried to imagine who this Norwegian woman was. If I went to the train station and arrived in Oslo and followed the directions, where would they take me?

I imagined a big house, with stairs up to the front door. Through the window I could see chandeliers, and a family sitting together. An elegant woman answers the door. She recognises me instantly. She embraces me.

'Kari, it's you. Never leave me again.'

Her husband, my father, comes to the door, a handsome man with kind eyes.

'Kari, my daughter … Come home to us at last.'

Then I remembered what the lady on the telephone had said: 'I think *she* should tell you about your father. It's not my place.'

What did she mean by that? My daydream now took a different shape. I imagined the same house. But this time, through the window I see my father sitting in a wheelchair, an invalid – some terrible accident has left him without the use of his legs.

Then, I have yet another vision of my father, this time as a rich businessman who's left my mother for his young secretary. He sits at a hotel bar, smoking a cigar, flirting with a woman in a red dress, while my mother is left to fend for herself in that big old house, raising the children on her own, cursing him for leaving her.

Or maybe none of these are true. Perhaps he's not in the picture at all. Maybe he's dead, killed in the war, and she mourns for him. Every night she prays as she kneels before his picture on the mantelpiece.

Then I imagined being on the same street, walking past the house with chandeliers and heading down a dark alleyway, towards a dilapidated building. The garden is overgrown with weeds. The windows are boarded up.

A man with a cigarette answers the door. He has bad teeth. He's wearing an old leather jacket. He reeks of nicotine. Inside women are walking around the house in short skirts and bad make-up. My mother, the whore, sits at the back of the room. She wears red lipstick and blue eye shadow. She denies knowing anything about me. The man hits her and they yell at each other. She cries, and I run away.

I played out all these scenarios in my head. I had to know which one, if any, was true.

The next day, I rang the hospital before my shift was due to start, and told Dagmar about the telephone call from The Red Cross, hoping she would understand why I hadn't been in work and would let me take some more time off.

'She says she knows who my real mother is. That I can go to meet her in Oslo. I don't know what to do.'

I thought Dagmar might be angry at me for missing shifts at the hospital. She hesitated for a moment.

'You must go,' she said. 'This is important. I'll cover for you. I'll say you've come down with the flu, and I won't allow you to be around the patients until it passes over.'

'Thank you, Sister Dagmar.'

I was about to hang up when Dagmar spoke again.

'Kari, I know this is hard. But either way, you have to know the truth. Be strong.'

I put down the phone. My suitcase was packed. Now all I had to do was go.

I didn't know how long I would be there. I didn't even know if the tickets and address would be at the train station like the woman had said. But I did know there was a train to Oslo that evening.

I took one last look at my apartment as I closed the door behind me.

My suitcase was heavy. I shifted it to my left hand as I made my way towards the train station.

The city seemed busier than usual. It was evening time and traffic was heavy. A boy was selling newspapers from a stall, calling out the headlines. People were dying in Vietnam; Frankfurt was holding a trial about Auschwitz; the Americans were outraged about something or other. It made me feel like the world was a dangerous place. I felt like turning back, but I kept going.

There were people everywhere at the station. I saw a big 'TICKET' sign and made my way towards the booth.

I only had 100 kroner, just enough to get me through a few days, or to book a cheap hotel if I needed to. It was my emergency fund. I hoped I wouldn't have to pay for the train ticket out of it.

The man at the desk had a blue uniform. 'Yes, Miss. What can I do for you?'

There was a queue forming behind me. I didn't know what to say, so I just said my name.

'Kari Andersson.'

I had heard a lady in front of me doing the same thing.

'Here you go,' he said, handing me the tickets in an envelope.

I wasn't sure where to go. I stood for a moment.

'Platform 4,' he said, winking.

I boarded the train and found a carriage. It was a night train. Somehow it seemed easier to make the journey in the dark. At least that way I would arrive in the morning. As soon as I was settled, I took out a book, desperate to take my mind off things. It was called *In the Waiting*

Room of Death, a Sven Stolpe novel that I was determined to finish. But I couldn't concentrate. My thoughts were somewhere else.

More people piled onto the train. I looked at the hemline of my dress to check it wasn't torn, no threads out of place. It looked fine.

I wondered what she would be like – my mother. I had a sweet tooth. I wondered if she did too. I wondered what she was doing right at that moment, and if she ever thought of me.

I heard a man arguing with someone in the corridor. I hoped I would be able to sleep on the train. Maybe it wasn't wise to travel alone. Maybe I should have told Simon and Valborg where I was going. I couldn't though. Most things I could tell them, but I couldn't tell them this. How could I tell them that I was searching for other parents? As though they weren't good enough. Like I didn't love them. But it wasn't that at all. Something in me just needed answers. I didn't want our lives in Malexander to be changed by this – by whatever discovery lay ahead in Oslo. And if I told them, I felt things would be different between us and that thought frightened me. I would have to keep this journey a secret.

The train was getting noisier as more people made their way through the aisle, searching for empty compartments. Two people stopped outside my carriage. One, a heavy lady in a black dress, huffed and puffed as she tried to manipulate her leather case through the aisle. The other was a young man, about my age. He caught me looking at him. I couldn't help wishing that the woman would sit down beside me, rather than the handsome stranger. He reminded me too much of Daniel. He motioned for her to take the seat. She smiled, and barged in through the door.

'Is this seat free?' she asked.

'Yes, of course,' I said, relieved, as I watched the young man carry on down the corridor.

'My name is Maria,' she said, as she sat across from me.

'Kari,' I said.

'It's a bit hot in here, don't you think?'

I reached up and opened the window.

'That's much better.'

I didn't feel up to conversation. I tried to look away, but she insisted on telling me about her journey. She too was headed for Oslo.

'I have a sister there. We're going to the opera on Tuesday.'

She didn't seem to mind if I joined in the conversation or not.

She took out a stack of ham and cheese sandwiches from her bag. 'Want one?'

'Oh, no thanks,' I said. But she chucked a sandwich into my lap nonetheless.

I sat up with a jolt. The last thing I needed was to ruin my dress. It had taken me so long to choose what to wear. I looked down at my lap, examining it for stains, but there were none. I relaxed, and tucked into the sandwich. I was actually glad of something to eat. In all the rush, I had forgotten to pack any food.

As I listened to Maria talking, I watched a glob of mayonnaise that hung from the bottom of her sandwich. Crumbs flew everywhere, but I couldn't look down at my dress again, for fear of being impolite. If there is one thing Valborg taught me it was to be polite, and if there was another, it was to be neat with your food.

We talked as the train continued through the night. It helped to distract me for a while, and before I knew it we were half way through the journey. I leaned my head against the window, and tried to get some sleep. The rocking of the train was soothing, as was the rhythm of the wheels on the track. I could hear Maria's deep breathing, and her occasional snore.

'Gothenburg Central!' announced Maria, waking me with a start. I was in a deep sleep.

'What?' I said. 'I'm going to Oslo!' I was panicking now, gathering my belongings from around the cabin.

'It's fine. We're just changing trains. The next train will bring us to Oslo.'

I felt disorientated. Part of me wished that I had taken the wrong train, and had to call this whole thing off.

I didn't have time to think though, as Maria edged me towards the door.

'Come on, the train is going to leave again. We have to get off!'

She dragged her suitcase back through the aisle, bumping and knocking as she went. I followed her, nodding at people apologetically, as we made our way off the train, just in the nick of time before it pulled out again. Back on the platform she threw her bag down, wiped the sweat from her forehead with her sleeve, and tried to catch her breath.

'Okay,' she said, 'Oslo, here we come.'

We made our way across the station, and boarded the train for Oslo.

'All aboard!' called out the conductor, and we were off.

A few hours later, we arrived in Oslo.

Maria and I said our goodbyes. I hadn't told her why I was going to Norway. I wouldn't have known what to say. I barely knew why I was going myself. Her sister was waving excitedly at her from the other side of the station and she hurried off to meet her. They looked so alike. I watched them for a moment, until they disappeared out of sight, and I was on my own again.

5

Åse

The train station in Oslo was busier than the one in Sweden. It felt strange to suddenly be in another country. Everything looked like it was a shade of grey. I looked around for an exit. I was still disorientated from lack of sleep. I didn't even know where I was supposed to go. I went to the bathroom and splashed water on my face.

This was a stupid idea, I thought, making my way back onto the platform. I looked around for the train to Linköping. I wanted to go home.

Just at that moment I felt a tap on my shoulder. It was a woman pushing a pram with a newborn baby. She wanted directions to somewhere in Oslo. She was speaking Norwegian, but I could understand her perfectly. It just took a little concentration. It surprised me how similar the languages were.

I shrugged. 'Sorry, I don't know,' I said, in my strongest Swedish accent, trying to show her that I was from another country and couldn't help her find her way. Her baby gurgled and we both turned to look at him. We smiled at each other, and she stopped an old man who was passing, who pointed her in the right direction. And then it occurred to me – I didn't know where I was going either. I remembered what the woman on the phone had said – that there would be a letter with the tickets to tell me where to go. I had been so worried about getting on the train, I hadn't thought about the next step. I took a deep breath and reached for the envelope in my coat pocket. There was a piece of paper inside, with a name and an address:

> *Åse Løwe*
> *Wessels gate 15*
> *Oslo*
> *Norway*

It looked strange. I couldn't make out if it was a street or a house number, or maybe an apartment block. 'Åse'. Was that my mother's name? Åse? It sounded foreign to me, so simple. Three letters.

And 'Norway' again. I thought of the form Father Mats had given me. Well, here I was at last.

I hailed a taxi. The driver was an elderly man with a cap. He barked something in Norwegian. He turned his head to look at me in the back seat, and it dawned on him that I was foreign. He spoke more slowly. I could understand him when he spoke slowly. He pointed to a map. I handed him the piece of paper I had. He looked at it, grunted, and put his foot down on the accelerator.

We made our way through the streets of Oslo. There was a lot of traffic, which seemed to infuriate the man with the cap. We stopped and started. He threw his arms to heaven and yelled things out the window that I couldn't understand.

Eventually, we pulled into a quiet street. The car stopped.

'Wessels gate,' he said, and waited for me to pay him.

I got out. Children were playing in the street. They looked poor. I wasn't going to find my house with chandeliers here. There was an old woman on the footpath. I caught myself looking at everyone, wondering if one of them was the Åse Løwe I'd come to find.

I paid the driver.

He took the money and pointed.

I turned to look. 'Thank …' But he was gone before I could finish.

In front of me was a tall, grey apartment block, with rows and rows of square windows. It looked dark and uninviting. There was an old gnarled tree that leaned towards the building casting a shadow across the entrance.

The taxi disappeared around the corner at the top of the street. I wanted to yell after the driver to stop so I could climb back into the car, and he could drive me all the way back to Simon and Valborg. But he didn't stop, and I didn't yell. Instead I stood there, rooted to the pavement.

People were looking over at me. I imagine they were wondering who the strange girl was, and why she was standing outside the apartment block.

Suddenly I was very nervous. I felt like I was going to get sick. I leaned against the tree, hoping no one from inside the building could see me.

I took deep breaths, and waited until I wasn't dizzy anymore. I closed my eyes to gather my thoughts so I could muster up the courage for what I had to do next.

People who are not adopted can never know what it's like. There's always a mystery inside you. All my life I felt like there was a room in my house that was locked. No one knew what was inside. No one talked about the room, or went near it. Sometimes at night I would feel it, drawing me towards it, pleading with me to turn the handle and look inside.

And here I was, just a few feet from the handle, about to turn it at last.

I stood up straight, fixed my hair and checked the address again. I watched the door numbers go up and up, until I knew I was coming close ... 13 ... 14 ... And there it was: a dark blue door with a brass '15'. The door I had been searching for all my life.

Once I knocked, there was no going back. I had to reconcile myself with that. And that there might be something on the other side I wouldn't want to see.

I looked around. A man two doors down stopped watering the potted plants on his doorstep, and stared at me.

I peered in through the window of number 15, checking for signs of life inside. I heard some shuffling. I was about to knock when the door opened.

A woman stood in the frame. Neither of us said a word. I looked at her. It was like gazing into a mirror. The woman in front of me was the image of me, but older. The same fair hair and blue eyes. It was like looking into my own future. We both stood still. She didn't smile. She just stared back at me. Then she pulled the door wide and stood aside.

I was in shock. I wanted to go back to where I came from and forget I had ever been here. In this place where all the whispering of old ladies from my childhood would be explained. I wanted to find Daniel and never mention this to anyone again. I wanted the safety of ignorance.

But I couldn't have it. Pandora's Box was open. There was nothing I could do. Almost in a dream, I leaned forward and stepped inside. And the woman, my mother, my real mother, shut the door behind me.

6

My mother

I cannot describe the feeling. It is as if I were in a dream, the type of dream you have when you're half awake and aware that you are dreaming. As though you were watching yourself from above.

I stood across from my mother. She was an elegant woman. More so than me. Though she seemed haggard somehow. She had the look of someone who had once been very beautiful. She looked like she was wearing her good clothes, making a special effort for the occasion. But there was something unnerving about her. Something unsettling. She leaned forward and touched my arm. My body froze, and she recoiled, just as quick, as though she felt she had no right. Maybe she hadn't. I didn't know how to feel. I had never had a blood relative before. I didn't know what you did when you met one, at 21 years of age.

I suddenly became aware that I was with a stranger. She invited me into the living room. I followed her in. Her furniture was old and worn. I sat down and tried to look around the room, but seem as though I wasn't looking.

The room was bare, without ornamentation, except for a framed photograph of a man on the mantelpiece.

She sat in the chair opposite me. She leaned forward and put her hand on my hand.

'Were they kind to you, Kari?'

'Yes,' I said.

Her eyes filled with tears, but none fell to her cheeks. Her eyes just glossed over, making them a startling shade of blue. It was strange to hear my name from her lips. She said it in such a familiar way, as though she had said it every day. But she had never called my name for dinner, had never whispered it as she tucked me into bed at night. She had never yelled it in anger. There were so many ways she had never said my name. It seemed almost like theft for her to say it now, as though she thought she had a right, a right to call me by my name, the name she had given me. How dare she try to steal it back now.

We talked about the weather. I know that seems strange. We didn't know what else we had in common. It made me sad. And as we talked of rain and of longer summer days, we watched each other. We said the words, but there was another conversation going on underneath. It was exhausting.

She asked if I would stay with her while I was in Oslo. She then asked if I'd like to go to bed. I had imagined this moment many times, and I had never thought that all I would want would be to sleep. I never knew just how draining it would be. How little there would be to say. I just wanted to shut my eyes and face another day tomorrow.

She motioned for me to follow her. It began to feel real

at last. I would stay the night, with this woman I had just met, this woman who was my mother.

I had always imagined that by finding my mother I would complete the picture of my life. But in reality, it only opened up more questions. I was there in the house with her, and I was still searching.

She stopped and held the door open. It was her bedroom.

I looked at her, but she shook her head. 'It's fine, I'm not tired. You get some sleep.' And then she left the room.

I felt my eyelids closing. I knew that sleep would come quickly. My body felt like it was shutting down. I curled up in the bed, clutching the pillow close to my chest. I fell into a deep sleep, only to be woken some time later by the sound of the wooden floor creaking. Someone was coming into the room. My mother. She shut the door behind her. I didn't move a muscle. I kept my eyes closed and listened for every movement, wondering what she would do next. I felt the bed dip and the spring under the mattress creak as she climbed in beside me. I could feel her lying there, close to me. She moved closer still. I could feel her feeling my presence, breathing me in. It hurt to feel her hurt. It was as though her body and mind were at odds. She couldn't communicate, but she wanted to be close to me. We lay, side by side, but there was a chasm between us, much bigger than those few inches of bed sheets. We were a world apart, and yet together. I shut my eyes, and hoped tomorrow would be easier.

The next morning I awoke again to the sounds of movement in the room. I opened my eyes, thinking for a moment I was back in Linköping. And then it dawned on me. It wasn't a dream. I was in a stranger's bedroom, in Oslo. Quietly, I turned and looked over at Åse. She was getting dressed. I watched the private moments of a woman I hardly knew. She reached her arms above her head to put on her blouse. As her body twisted I saw an ugly scar across her chest on the flesh around her bra. I shut my eyes, afraid that she might see me watching her. She left the room, but the scar stayed imprinted on my mind.

꧁꧂

I spent two weeks in that apartment. And in all that time, she refused to talk about my father. Every time I tried to ask, an energy filled the room that told me not to.

Each day she grew more and more silent. The space between us in the bed grew bigger every night. Her vulnerability started to feel like something else, more like resentment. The silence was heavy. Whatever niceties were there in the beginning were gone now. I was no longer a guest, I was an intruder.

Her gaze was distant. She looked that way a lot of the time. A vacant look, as though she was not in the room. As though her mind was elsewhere. Or nowhere.

'We're going on a journey,' she told me as I sat down to breakfast. 'Pack your bags tonight. We leave tomorrow.'

I was about to ask where we were going when she spoke again.

'You have his eyebrows. You remind me of him,' she said. 'He was not a nice man.' She said it without my asking, or thinking of asking. Just like that, and she never said anything of him again. My father. I went to bed that night, and before I turned out the lights, I watched myself in the mirror in the bedroom. I could see my mother in me now, but there was still something missing. I was a mix of two people. Everyone is. And the rest was still a mystery. I stared at my eyebrows – the closest I would ever come to knowing my father. What did that mean – 'he was not a nice man'? What part of him was me? I had Simon's accent, and his turn of phrase. I had grown to be like him. Through mimicry, not biology. I was Simon's daughter. But whatever part of me was Simon was masking the other part of me. The part that was my German father.

The next day I woke to a loud knock. 'We leave in 20 minutes.'

She told me we were going to visit some of my mother's family in the south. We were taking the train. I was anxious at the thought of it. I had barely come to terms with meeting one blood relative. I didn't know if I had it in me to meet more.

We sat beside each other on the train, our elbows lightly touching, without a word passing between us. When she didn't know I was looking I watched her staring out the window. I wondered what she was thinking. She seemed to carry so much pain with her. I think I reminded her of the war – of everything that had gone wrong with her life. I think she wished I had never come. And then other times she seemed to want me there. She was in two minds, all the time. There were still so many questions she hadn't answered, so much I needed to know. She never seemed to want to talk about it. About my father or why I had been given up for adoption. But at least she was trying, I thought. It must have been hard for her, me suddenly appearing back in her life. No one prepares you for something like this. No one tells you how to do it right.

As the train came to a halt, she suddenly became energised. She gathered her things, and said, without looking at me, 'We are going to introduce you as my friend. You are just my friend Kari. Is that understood?'

It felt like she had kicked me in the stomach. 'We' – like it was something we had decided together. Like we were a team. But we weren't a team. We were the opposite. That's what she was really telling me. I couldn't believe she was bringing me to see her family, and she still didn't want to tell them I was her daughter. It felt like she was disowning me again. Like she was ashamed of me. In that moment I disliked her more than anyone I had ever met. Her words weighed heavily on me. And I was angry at myself for going along with it all. More secrets. More lies.

'Kari, you must promise me …'

'I promise,' I said, defeated.

I had no choice. I was complicit now.

She leaned on me to push herself up out of the seat. She had suffered from tuberculosis of the hip, and it made her joints stiff, making her seem older than her years. We made our way out of the station. It was a sleepy little town, but Åse walked the streets like she was familiar with them. I wondered if she had grown up there. We got on a bus and Åse told me we were going to a nursing home to see her mother, my real grandmother. I didn't know if

I could lie or not – whether I had it in me to be part of this conspiracy. More than two decades had passed and still Åse could not take responsibility. She could not call me her own. I was still a stranger to her. I wondered why I had come at all. But if she didn't want me in her life, why was she bringing me to see her family? It was all so confusing.

'Here we are,' she said. She got up, and started making her way towards the front of the bus. I remained seated.

'Kari!' People were looking over now. Reluctantly, I followed her off the bus. Across the street was an old whitewashed building, with a lawn outside, and flower beds. We made our way through the metal gate, and up the garden path, where we were greeted by a nurse. She seemed to know my mother. After she took our coats, she led us into a big open room.

All the chairs were placed in a horseshoe shape. The old people sat, side by side, drained, I thought, of the colour of their youth. Some were slumped over, dozing, while others were knitting, or talking to pass the time. There was a smell of must and of scrambled eggs. I could hear the noise of clattering plates from the kitchen, and the squeak of wheelchairs and the sounds of heavy doors opening and closing.

I looked around, wondering which of the old ladies was my grandmother. They all looked up as we walked in, each hoping for a visitor, except one. She had a cane by her chair, and she stared down at the floor. Åse knelt down beside her.

'Mama,' Åse said, her voice softening to a near whisper.

She put her hand on the woman's arm, and the old lady's face lit up with a smile.

'Åse, is that you?'

'Yes, Mama.' I could see they were close.

'Who is with you, Åse?' The old woman was blind.

'This is my friend, Kari, from the city. Kari, meet Anna, my mother.'

Åse locked eyes with me, waiting to pounce if I made one false move.

'Anna, nice to meet you,' I said.

What a strange coincidence, I thought, that she too was called Anna – like Simon's mother, my other grandmother in Sweden. But this was a world away from the grandmother of my childhood – with the long, flowing hair and the chocolate cakes. In that moment I longed to be back in Malexander with her and all her old neighbours who knew me and loved me, and were always glad to see me coming.

I put out my hand to shake hers. I had never met a blind person before. I wasn't sure what to do. But Anna was a gentle woman. I could see it in her smile.

'Can I touch your face?' she said. 'I want to know what you look like.'

Åse looked nervous.

I leaned forward, and Anna moved her hands across my face. I closed my eyes, and as her fingers traced the contours of my nose and cheeks, I felt her pause, just for a moment, and I knew what she was thinking. How could it be that my face was so like Åse's? In that moment, we were connected, she and I. For just a moment I felt connected to my maternal grandmother, and all the people who came before her, to make me – me. I felt a surge of defiance come over me. I wanted to tell her who I was. She knew already. I was sure of it. So why were we both playing Åse's game? I felt my mouth open to say something, and then, just as quickly, I closed it again. I opened my eyes and caught a glimpse of Åse's face. It was strained with fear. She had lived a life of secrets and I now had the power to bring it all crashing down, in just one sentence. But I stayed silent.

Anna broke the silence.

'What a beautiful young woman,' she said. 'How old are you, Kari?'

'I'll be 21 in September.'

'Mother, have you eaten?' Åse interrupted, wanting to turn to more practical matters, before her mother had time to do the calculations in her head, to tally up the years. She signalled for a nurse to adjust Anna's pillows.

'Lovely weather outside today,' said the nurse, tending to Anna. 'The garden's coming along beautifully.'

I looked at the tulips, just visible through the window. I wondered if this meeting would be different if Anna could see.

They talked over the next hour, of Norway, and Oslo. I tried to stay quiet. I knew nothing of Norway, and I knew if I spoke, the secret would unravel. I wondered if my Swedish accent gave me away.

∾⚘∾

That evening we were to stay with Alf, Åse's brother, who lived in the same town. Just when I thought things couldn't get any stranger, Åse said she had something to tell me. We were walking towards Alf's house.

'Kari, you might meet a boy here ...'

'What?' I was exhausted from the day, and wondered what else she had in store for me.

'You might meet a boy, a little older than you, at Alf's house. You mustn't tell him who you are. You have to keep your promise. Do you understand?'

'Yes ... I've been keeping your secret,' I said.

'Good.'

'Who is he, the boy?'

She was nervous.

I tried again. 'Is he related to me?' I felt like she was about to tell me something.

'He's your brother,' she said.

'My ...' I couldn't even say the word.

'Yes, your brother. Your half-brother.'

'What do you mean, my brother?' I stopped walking.

I had always dreamed of having a brother.

She was a few paces ahead when she realised I had stopped walking along beside her. 'Kari, come on.'

'Tell me,' I said.

'That man, in the photograph, on the mantelpiece in Oslo ...'

'Yes?' I said.

'He was my first love. He was killed in the war. We had a baby boy ...'

'Was that man ... my father?'

'No. He wasn't. He died a long time before I met ...'

'Met ... my father?'

'Yes.'

'What's his name, my brother?'

'Per,' she said, growing suddenly impatient by this inquisition. 'But Kari, you have made a promise. Things will be a lot worse if you tell him.'

We reached the house. A man opened the door, and introduced himself as Alf. The atmosphere was strained. He showed us to our bedroom, and invited us to come downstairs to dinner. His wife, Elsa, was cooking in the kitchen. I kept looking around for signs of Per.

We were silent around the dinner table, eating soup and bread, when I heard the front door open. I tensed up. Per, I thought. It could be him. There was a shuffling in the hall, and then a young man walked into the room. Per. I knew immediately. He was tall and handsome and strong. All the things I imagined a brother would be.

He looked surprised to see us sitting there in the kitchen.

'Hello,' he said, looking towards me. I looked at Åse. She was looking up at him. 'Hello,' Åse said. And then he left the room.

My heart was pounding. I wanted to run after him and tell him I was his sister. He was my brother. I looked at the faces around the table. The atmosphere was heavy. No one said anything. I heard the front door open and close again. Per was gone.

I caught my uncle and aunt studying me with their eyes, when they thought I wasn't looking. I wondered why Åse had brought me here. It was as though she wanted to show them, wanted to show me off, but without actually saying anything. They must have known. They must have realised. Åse and I looked too alike for it to be a coincidence, but we all kept up the pretence.

The next day we took the train back to Oslo. Back to the confines of Åse's apartment. I felt tired most of the time. Sometimes it felt natural to be with her, and at other times she made it almost impossible. She could suck all the air out of the room. She was depressed. I know that now.

That night, as we sat in the living room, she tried to tell me why she was the way she was. I felt she wanted me to know that she had been a different person once, that she was not always this way.

'It was the war,' she said, and left it hanging in the air. She looked at the photograph of Per's father on the mantelpiece.

'Why didn't he speak to you?' I asked.

'Who?'

'Per. He didn't speak to you.'

'He … He doesn't want to see me.'

'What do you mean? Isn't he your son?'

'He was raised by my brother. He doesn't, he can't … Look, it's complicated. It's all so complicated. It's nothing to do with you.'

'Nothing to do with me? I was your daughter. How did I end up in an orphanage in Sweden? How did that happen? You abandoned me, just like you did Per. Who did you give me to? Why won't you tell me?'

'I didn't abandon you. You were taken.'

'I don't believe you. Taken by who?'

She just stared at me. Silence again. And then she turned her head away.

I stood up and left the room. I got into bed. I couldn't take this anymore. I still didn't know what happened in the first three years of my life, and how I ended up an orphan in Sweden.

And to think Per was out there all along, living in Norway – the brother I had always wanted, the one I never had, because of her. I had grown up as an only child, always longing for a brother. I thought back to my childhood days in Malexander, when I had invented an imaginary brother, Peter. And yet, all those years, when I was chasing Peter through the fields, my real brother, Per, was out there, and I never knew him.

That night as I felt Åse getting into bed, I flinched at the thought of her beside me. I felt angry at her for still keeping secrets from me, when I had come all this way. I felt like she had robbed me of so much. Of my identity. And of my brother too. I tried to hold the memory of that moment in my mind, when I had seen Per walk through the door. I closed my eyes, and hoped that somehow he knew I was his sister. At least fate had brought us together, if only for a moment, I thought. And I drifted off to sleep.

The next morning I packed up my things, and wondered how we would say goodbye. I wanted nothing more than to leave. I couldn't take the silence anymore. I needed noise and energy, and conversation. I needed to figure out what all this meant.

I longed to be back on the train, on my own again,

heading in the direction of home. Towards Daniel. And Linköping. And Sweden. Thoughts were flooding my mind. I had met my mother. That's what I had come to do, but I still had so many questions. I kept thinking of the man in the photograph, Per's father, and wondering who my father was. But I knew she would never tell me. I needed to get away.

As I stood in the hall, ready to leave again, I wondered how she could have left me when I was a baby. Or allowed me to be taken. I turned to look at her. If this were Malexander, we would hug to say goodbye. I waited to see if she would hug me. She didn't.

'Goodbye,' she said.

'Goodbye. It was … nice … to meet you.' I paused. 'Thank you, for …'

She looked down at the floor.

'For agreeing to meet me …'

'You're welcome,' she said.

And I walked out the door. It was all too hard. I had told her Simon and Valborg needed me to return and that I promised I would come back to help them on the farm. What was one more lie in a lifetime of lies?

7

A new beginning

Back in Linköping I felt like a weight was lifted from me. I telephoned Daniel when I arrived, and we met that very night. The argument and childishness of our last encounter had quickly been forgotten. He asked me all about my journey, and about my mother.

'What was she like?'

'I don't know,' I said, 'she was ... different. I don't know.'

I didn't want to talk of her. I felt guilty at the mention of her. I tried to put her out of my mind as the days and weeks passed, but sometimes at night I would imagine I was back in that apartment in the middle of Oslo and that she was sleeping next to me. I could hear the ticking of the old clock in the hall, pounding out time in a house of silence.

But during the day, it was as though she never existed, as though I had never been to Oslo. It was the only way I could cope – to put it out of my mind. I tried to focus on Daniel, and the things I loved about Linköping. Time marched on, and Daniel and I moved in together. It all happened nearly by accident. My flatmate Yvonne told me that she was getting married, and she and her husband wanted to live in the apartment as a couple, and since she had lived there first, she laid claim to it, which meant I had to go. I didn't argue. Yvonne could be stubborn when she wanted to be, and I knew she would win out in the end. When I told Daniel I needed to find somewhere to live, his eyes lit up.

'Live with me.'

'Are you sure? It's not too soon?'

'Kari … live with me.'

It was just that simple with him. He was sure, so he made me feel sure. It felt like the right thing to do. I moved into his apartment the following week. It was a man's place, full of old shoes and newspaper cuttings, but little by little, as the months went by, I added a potted plant here and a tablecloth there, and slowly but surely it began to feel like home.

The months passed quickly, and they turned to years, and we were happy together. We spent our days working, our evenings talking and cooking, and the weekends with friends and family. We didn't have much by way of money, just enough to get by, but it was one of the best times of my life. I felt so free, like anything was possible, so long as we were together.

One day after work, Daniel and I were in the sitting room eating our dinner, when out of nowhere he put down his fork, looked at me, and said, 'Kari, I think we should get married.' Like he was asking me to pass the salt or something.

'Daniel ... are you sure? This sounds crazy.'

'I've never been surer of anything in my life,' he said, and kissed my hand.

I froze. I had imagined this moment so many times, and now that it was here, I didn't know what to say. I moved my lips, but no sound came out. Daniel looked at me, his eyes wide, vulnerable, waiting for an answer. I nodded my head, smiling. Then he suddenly swept me up in his arms, dropping the cutlery, and carried me into the bedroom. And just like that, the decision was made.

∞

A few months later we got married in a place called Västervik, a seaside town not far from Linköping. It was a summer's day. Everything was organised, and it was just the way we wanted it.

We walked up the aisle together, hand in hand, between the rows of family and friends. I felt he was the love of my life. Everything felt perfect.

Daniel's father filmed the ceremony, and later we laughed, watching the film. He captured one moment, when we didn't know he was filming. It's just a second or two. It looks as though Daniel is chasing after me. The train of my dress is caught in something, and he runs after me to help me. It's the way I always think of him, trapped in that moment in time, chasing after me, wanting to set me free. He had a way of making even the colours of the day look brighter – the green of the grass, and the blue of the sky. I could smell the fresh air, and feel the warmth of the sun on my skin. It was like all my senses were heightened when he was around. I can still hear the church bells.

After the wedding, when all the noise of family and friends had died down and we were on our own, I had time to think. I wondered if I had made the right decision, not to invite Åse. I couldn't have imagined her there. Somehow she didn't fit the picture. How would I have introduced her even? As my friend, as she had introduced me? I wrote her a letter a few days later and told her that I had got married, that I was happy and that everything had gone well. I didn't want to hurt her, but I couldn't think what else to do. I felt somehow I owed it to her to tell her about the wedding, at least. I don't know why.

Daniel and I moved to Norrköping, a town just north of Linköping, a few weeks after the wedding. It all happened suddenly. Daniel got a job at the university in Norrköping. It was a good job. It would pay well. And it wasn't as though we had to move very far. It was only half an hour's drive away. It seemed the sensible thing to do, so we packed up all our things and put them in the back of the car. Our whole lives in a few boxes, I thought, as I closed the boot.

'It'll be an adventure,' Daniel said.

Part of me was hesitant. I wasn't sure about leaving the hospital. I was good at my job and I had made friends, good friends, there. I felt like things were finally settled in Linköping. But Valborg reminded me that I was Daniel's wife and it was my duty to go with him. We were only going to the next city. I knew it wasn't far away, but it felt strange walking away from our home, the world we had made with one another. I tucked the key under the mat for the last time.

I watched the familiar buildings and trees disappear through the rear-view mirror, as we journeyed towards Norrköping and our new life together. Daniel could see I was uneasy. Change came easier to him. He moved with things. In some ways we were polar opposites, and sometimes I felt I had to overcompensate for his lack of worry. He switched on the radio and a familiar song came on. He nudged me as he sang along, drumming the rhythm with his fingers against the wheel. He made me laugh and soon I found myself singing too.

We arrived at our new apartment. It was all ready for us. Daniel had organised it through a friend in Norrköping who said he could help me to get a job at Ericsson, the communications company.

'Here we are,' said Daniel, as we pulled into the driveway. I tried to look happy but there were so many thoughts going on inside my head as I looked around, taking it all in. The building was more modern than our old apartment block. It would take a lot of getting used to. I'd only ever known life with Daniel in our home in Linköping. I never said it out loud, but I was worried that maybe we only worked as a couple in that apartment, and that in other circumstances we might be different people. I knew I was being childish, but I just couldn't help wondering what life would be like starting all over again in a new job, and a new neighbourhood, with a whole new city to navigate. I was excited, but I was nervous too.

During our first few weeks there I felt unsettled. I was moody with him, impatient. The more he said things would be okay, the more I came up with reasons why they wouldn't. I knew I was being unreasonable. There was just something playing on my mind, that wouldn't let me be at ease.

The weeks passed, and one morning I woke up feeling queasy. I was pregnant.

I wanted to be absolutely sure before I told Daniel. I let another month go by. Daniel came home from work one day and I decided it was time.

He could usually tell when I was hiding something. But somehow I had managed to keep it secret. When he walked through the door he seemed to sense something was up.

He put his arms around me, and hugged me from behind.

'Kari ... there's something you're not telling me. You haven't stopped smiling since I got home. What is it?'

'Sit down,' I said. 'I have something to tell you.' Daniel ... I'm ...'

'Are you pregnant?'

I nodded, and he leaped forward to hug me. Then he pulled back, worried he would upset my now fragile, pregnant body.

'Kari, this is wonderful! It's the best news! I can't believe it!'

It made me happy to see him happy.

I rang Valborg and Simon, and told them we were coming to visit. I wanted to tell them in person. I wanted to tell the world I was pregnant. There are so many things in your life you can hide, so many secrets you can keep, but it's almost as though nature wants everyone to know when you are pregnant – your stomach gets bigger and bigger, and hardens like a drum – a proclamation to the world that you're making a new life.

It felt odd though, too. I don't think I'd ever really processed what it all meant. I had thought about babies, and children, and the future, the same as anyone does. But it was only months later that it became real to me, what was happening. One night Daniel and I were lying in bed, ready to go to sleep. I was eight months pregnant at the time, and every day felt like the baby might come – then and there – in a shop, or walking down the street. I felt like I could give birth any moment. I was at bursting point.

When I lay down flat on the bed, the bump seemed bigger. I could feel the baby moving a lot now, as though he were getting impatient; he was ready for the world. Daniel had the side light on, and was flicking through an old maths book. He must have read that book a hundred times. All of a sudden I felt a jolt, and with a reflex, kicked out my leg and hit Daniel.

'Ouch!' he yelled.

'Ouch!' I yelled.

He threw the book down, and turned to me.

'What's going on? Are you alright?'

I was breathing heavily, pursing my lips. 'Huu huuu huuh huuh.' Deep, sharp breaths.

'Is it time?'

'I don't know,' I said. And we both looked at the bump as though it was a bomb ready to explode. One false move and we were done for. My breathing slowed, and we both relaxed. A false alarm. We tried to calm ourselves, but our eyes stayed fixed on my stomach.

I had pulled up my nightdress, and my skin was nearly the same colour as the sheets – milk white from the winter months. Daniel was rubbing my belly in circular motions. And almost as though he knew his dad was saying hello, a little fist appeared through the skin. We both gasped. It was like an alien creature, reaching through the shell of my stomach. And we looked at each other, and laughed in disbelief. This was really happening. I still think of that day as the first day we met Roger.

And sure enough, a few weeks later he was born. Ten fingers, ten toes, and a little button nose. My perfect Roger.

He felt so fragile. I've never been delicate. I was always clumsy, dropping things, and breaking things wherever I went. I clasped my fingers tight beneath the arch of his back and cradled him in my arms. I promised him I would never drop him or break him. I promised him I would never let him go.

Daniel was standing beside me. I passed the baby carefully into his arms and I watched my husband's face light up.

That night we brought Roger home for the first time. We tucked him into a cot that Daniel had made by hand. He had spent hours carving out just the right pieces of wood and putting them together. I think it was his way of feeling useful. He could use up his nervous energy. At night time I could hear him hammering and sawing in the next room, the dim light visible beneath the bedroom door. I found the noises soothing. It was a reminder that we were in it together. I think it gave him purpose too – made him feel like he could contribute, while I incubated our future.

That night as Roger lay sleeping in the cot, I smiled at the imperfections: holes in the wood where misplaced nails had been prised out, the bars of the cot not quite aligned, leaning in different directions, standing to attention like drunken soldiers. Daniel was no carpenter, but I knew what it meant to him to create a safe home for our baby. I went to the window, pushed back the net curtain, and looked up at the moon. I wanted to hold that moment. That true happiness. I wanted to remember that feeling. But it didn't last long. Suddenly, Roger began to cry.

I moved to pick him up. He was wailing now. I made shushing sounds and rocked him back and forth, but the crying just got louder and more frantic. I felt desperate now, pacing around the room, holding him close to my body.

'Everything's okay ... Mama's here ... shhhh shhh shhh.' But as I tried to comfort him, I could feel tears roll down my cheeks. Daniel walked into the room, his sleepy eyes adjusting to the light.

'Is he alright?'

'I don't know what's wrong with him,' I said as I thrust the baby into his arms and walked out of the room.

'Kari, what's the matter?'

Daniel looked confused. Just moments earlier we had watched our newborn baby sleeping peacefully as the moonlight streamed in through the window.

I got back into bed. My mother abandoned me when I was a baby. She had not wanted me. What if I was like her? What if I was not the mothering kind? I didn't know how to stop him crying. What use was I to him? All these thoughts were racing through my mind.

I heard Daniel calming the baby in the next room, singing a Swedish lullaby. I closed my eyes, and pretended he was singing to me. The wailing turned to a gurgle, and then to silence. The light switch was flicked, and I could hear footsteps approach the bed.

'Kari, talk to me,' Daniel whispered.

I didn't make a sound. I held my breath. He knew I was awake. But I didn't want him. I didn't want anyone.

I woke, hours later, to Daniel's voice. 'Kari.' The voice was stern now, impatient, annoyed.

'Kari, our child needs feeding.' It was morning time. I had slept the whole night. I pulled myself up out of bed, and went to the bathroom to splash cold water on my face.

What had come over me?

I knew Daniel had to go to college for a meeting. He had been working on a paper for months, and one of the professors wanted to meet with him to discuss his findings. I knew it was important to him. I heard him moving around the kitchen. I walked in, cradling Roger, and sat at the kitchen table.

I could feel Daniel's eyes on me. I opened my dressing gown and pulled Roger close to my breast to feed him. It hurt a little as he tugged at my nipple. I winced.

'Kari, I have to go for a few hours. Will you be alright to look after Roger?'

Already I had given him reason to doubt me.

'We'll be fine.'

He gathered his books and walked over to me, bent down, and kissed me on the forehead.

'I'll be back soon.'

I closed my eyes, and thanked God for Daniel, as I heard him make his way down the stairs. I felt so blessed that a man like that would make his way back home to me. I looked at Roger and knew that those games in my mind were nothing but a fantasy. I would be a good mother, I decided then and there. He was the most important thing I would ever do. He was my life. My Roger.

And from that moment on we were happy – the three of us. Our own little family. And I was able for it. Able for parenthood. It was exhilarating. You always hope you can be a good mother, but it is only in doing it that you find out for sure. Being a parent is funny like that. You don't get a practice round. We had our off days, but there were more good days than bad, and we laughed a lot, the three of us. And a lot of important things happened.

Somehow, before we knew it, Roger was one year old. We had a party in the apartment for his birthday and invited some of the children from the building. I'll never forget that day. All the children were sitting around in a circle, when Roger got to his feet and stumbled over to the girl next to him. His first steps. We all gasped.

'Roger! What a boy!' Daniel looked ecstatic. He took Roger's hand and helped him walk around the room. I felt teary watching them. I was so proud.

I had no idea then just how different things would be just one year later.

8

What a difference a year makes

In 1971, when Roger was two, it happened. The thing that you fear more than anything. When the doctor asks you to sit down, and he has that look, and he makes sure you have a glass of water beside you. These are not good signs.

Daniel had suddenly become ill. I had rushed him to hospital where they took him in to do some tests. I was called in to get the results. For his sake, I will not go into the details of his illness here, as I know it was a time of great suffering for him.

'Your husband is very sick. I'm sorry, but there's no other way to say this. We don't think he will get better anytime soon.'

I felt like someone had punched me. I didn't want to believe it.

I thought of the 'Baby's First Years' book that we had bought together, that was waiting to be filled with memories.

Only the week before, we had talked of how we would spend Christmas. And now, the thought of Christmas terrified me.

'I have nursing experience. I can look after him at home,' I said.

The doctor looked at me.

'But I believe you have a small child.'

'Yes, Roger.'

'I don't think you quite understand. Your husband will need full-time care for a while. As will your child, naturally. You won't be able to do both. We can care for Daniel in the hospital, where he will be properly looked after. Around the clock care. That's the level of attention that he will get here. How would you manage that?'

'I would manage.'

'You can't look after both of them. Your child would have to be looked after by relatives or by someone else. Perhaps social services could take your child for a period of time. We could look into that for you, if that's what you want.'

I stared at him. I couldn't believe what he was asking of me. To choose between my husband and my son. The two people I loved most.

'I don't understand what you are saying.'

'I'm saying you have options, choices. But you can't choose both. It has to be one or the other.'

If I was granted a wish at that second, I would have wished to go back to Linköping. To the way things were. To those simple, carefree days.

But I realised that that was a world without Roger.

I tried to think what was the right thing to do.

No matter what happened, I would let down someone I loved.

They say that time stands still when you are faced with some life-changing event, and that is how it felt, facing the doctor in that consulting room. It felt like hours, even though it must have been only seconds.

I thought of Simon and what he would do. I thought of the times he held my hand when I was a child, and made me feel safe.

I thought of my mother – she had made a decision long ago to give me to strangers, to abandon me. I couldn't do that to Roger. I couldn't be my mother.

'But what would happen to Daniel?'

'We will look after him. You can visit.'

It was the most difficult decision I have ever had to make. But deep down, I knew what was right. I was a mother first. I had to protect our family's future.

'Okay,' I said. 'Roger stays with me.'

'That's settled then.'

He handed me a piece of paper, with an address.

'This is where Daniel will be looked after. We'll need you to sign the papers. Tomorrow, around noon.'

All so clinical. And yet, our lives were turned upside down.

❧

The next day, I walked the long, winding driveway up to the hospital. I thanked God Roger was too young to know what was happening. I hoped he wouldn't be able to remember this. I wished for Daniel to come back to us, to get better again, but they told me that was not going to happen for a long time.

I hoped against logic that things would change. That things would go back to the way they were. I looked after the baby at home. It was a very stressful time.

I wanted Daniel to get better. But as the months passed, things seemed to change between us. I do not know why. I tried to talk to him, to tell him it would be alright. That things would get better. It seemed to make him worse. I think I reminded him of everything he was missing out on. Of life at home, with us. Life as a family.

We grew more and more distant. I still cannot speak of that time. The memory is just so painful. Some things you can't choose in life. I know deep down we still loved each other, but we weren't good together anymore. I felt helpless and he felt hopeless. Daniel became very detached from me. I think he did it out of love. I have to think that. That he didn't want to hold us back. So one day, we came to another decision. We talked it over. We signed the papers, and we were divorced. I felt numb. How quickly lives can change.

I walked that same long, winding driveway. No longer a married woman. I worried if we had done the right thing. I still yearned for him. I wanted to know how he was feeling, every minute of the day. Suddenly life was thrown into uncertainty. Nothing would ever be the same again.

I can see now that it was the right thing to do. That we weren't meant to be. Maybe we had rushed into things too quickly. Still so young. Maybe we were never going to be good together in the long run. Because when things got tough, we fell apart. That happens sometimes to couples.

I just never thought it would happen to us. Maybe there are things we could have done differently. You will always think that in life. Looking back. But you cannot change what is done.

You think of the promises you've made. The vows. But sometimes these things don't last forever. I felt empty for a long time after that. It was like a wound in my heart. I lost the man I loved. And yet I didn't have time to stop and think, to mourn the relationship. I had a child to raise. We both loved Roger. He was the best thing that ever happened to us. And whatever Roger would become, that was my responsibility now. I would raise our child.

I packed my bags. I knew what had to be done. I sat on the bed, in what had once been our bedroom, the room we had once shared. It held so many memories. Daniel's mother, who had come to visit, came into the room and sat beside me. She put her arm around me. She could see how much I was suffering, and the guilt I felt for leaving.

And then, she said something that I still treasure. I will always thank her for what she said next.

'Kari, you need to think of Roger now. That little boy. That's all that matters.'

'I just don't know if I'm strong enough to do this on my own,' I said.

She took my hand.

'You'll never be on your own, Kari. I'll be there. I promise. He's my grandchild.'

I still do not know how she had the strength to do that, to think of me, when she must have been hurting. She gave me strength. She released me from my promise to Daniel.

Because there was a bigger promise to keep. The day I gave birth to Roger, I promised never to let him go. I had to keep that promise, every day.

She could see my heart was breaking.

'I know it feels like the end,' she said, 'but it's not. You're young, Kari. I know you'll find love again.'

Her eyes welled with tears. 'But for now, we must think of Roger.'

9

Raising Roger

I moved back to Linköping. I drove that same road we had travelled together when we moved to Norrköping, only this time I was going in the opposite direction – like life was in rewind – going back again. But now it was just me and our baby. I couldn't bear to be in that apartment in Norrköping anymore. There were reminders of Daniel everywhere. Reminders of the life we would never have together – the one we'd planned.

I went back to my old job at the hospital. Dagmar was very understanding. I found a cheap apartment. It was just big enough for the two of us, but it was easy to heat, and there was a woman nearby who minded Roger during the day. No one prepares you for life as a single mother. It's definitely not the way things are supposed to be. Two hands just aren't enough when you're trying to balance work, home, and raising a child. Sometimes it all got too much, but for the most part, we managed. We were becoming a team, Roger and I. And he was growing quickly, and before I knew it, he was three years old. The age I was when I was adopted, I thought, as I hugged him close to me.

I talked to him all the time. You don't have adult company when you're a single parent, so you tell your child everything.

Sometimes I worried I wasn't enough for him. But in my times of doubt it was like Roger could sense what I was thinking. At just the right moment he would look up at me with those big eyes of his and laugh, to tell me everything would be fine, in a way that only Roger could. It made me laugh too, and it reminded me I couldn't take myself too seriously.

As he got bigger, and developed his own personality, I looked for signs of Daniel – facial expressions and quirks. It made me feel like some part of him was still there. Somehow we got by, Roger and I. I was determined to give him a happy childhood. I wanted to make things normal for him, or as normal as they could be. I worked day shifts at the hospital and looked after Roger in the evenings. We spent our weekends together, going to the park, feeding the ducks, and visiting Simon and Valborg on the farm. I couldn't believe how quickly he was growing.

When he was four, I found a playgroup for him, near the apartment. On the first day I dropped him off, I watched him playing with the other children, and I knew that I would do anything for him. I wanted so much for Roger to have all the things I never had. But, seeing him with other kids, I felt bad that I couldn't give him a brother or sister to play with.

It made me think of my brother, Per. I wondered what

he was doing. Where he was. It was at times like this I wondered what it would be like to have a sibling to lean on.

Life was hectic. Lately, though, something else was happening that I was trying to ignore. I had been getting dizzy spells, when my heartbeat would quicken.

I would breathe deeply for a moment or two, until it passed. But it was happening more and more. I tried to convince myself I just had a bad flu. Or it was exhaustion. I didn't have time to be sick. We had bills to pay, and someone had to look after Roger.

One day, as I was clearing some of the cups into the sink in the nurses' room, I fell. It's the last thing I remember – a clatter of cups falling on the floor, breaking into pieces. I blacked out and woke in a hospital bed. Bleary-eyed, I tried to make out the shapes around me. Valborg was sitting beside me. She called for a doctor. I didn't know what was happening.

'She's awake!' she called. She looked so happy. I had never seen her like that before.

I tried to lift my arms. I couldn't. Nothing would move. I panicked. What was wrong with my body? The doctor put his hand on my forehead.

'Welcome back,' he said.

Welcome back? What did that mean? They told me I had been unconscious for several days. I had a blood disease – porphyria. I could hear their words, but I was too exhausted to take in what they meant. I just wanted to close my eyes and go back to sleep.

They cared for me at the hospital and the days passed and turned to weeks. The doctors said they didn't know what they could do to help. People either got stronger or they didn't. There was no cure for porphyria. We just had to wait and see. Roger was being looked after by Simon and Valborg. What kind of curse, I thought, for both of Roger's parents to get ill, so soon after one another.

At least I knew he was in good hands with his grandparents. But that couldn't last forever. I needed so badly to get better so that I could look after him. As the days went by I hoped I would get stronger, but it only seemed to get worse.

A doctor took my temperature. I looked up at him, hopeful.

'Sorry, Kari, it's not good.'

I felt weak. I slept all day and it never seemed enough.

One day I woke to voices arguing around me. I opened my eyes and saw Daniel's mother there. She was arguing with one of the doctors. It felt comforting to know she was there. She was the kind of woman who would fight for you.

The doctor turned to me. 'Kari, your mother-in-law wants to take you to see a healer. I cannot stand over this decision. I cannot see what good it would do to disturb you. You shouldn't leave the hospital.'

'Let her take me,' I said. 'Please.'

I wanted nothing more than to be away from the hospital.

Daniel's mother was what I needed. She gave me the sense that Daniel was there – that a part of him was coming to my rescue.

We set off from Linköping and travelled for hours through the Swedish countryside, until we reached an area of dense woodland. Daniel's father was driving. When we arrived, he lifted me from the car, and carried my limp body through the forest. We arrived at a small run-down cottage, deep in the woods. There was a wheelbarrow and bits of firewood outside. Daniel's mother knocked on the door.

I wondered where we were. What if this is the last day of my life, I thought. What if this is where I die.

'Come in,' said a voice.

We went inside.

Held in Daniel's father's arms, all I could see was the roof of the cottage – the high beams and thatch. The room was warm. I could hear the crackle of a fire. They tried to sit me up in a wooden chair, but I was too limp, so they lay me on the table instead.

I didn't have the strength to hold my own body weight. It's only then that I saw the old man. He had wild hair, and a long, knotted beard.

'You must leave her here with me,' he said to Daniel's parents.

'But …' Daniel's mother was ready to argue.

'No, I must insist. She'll be safe here. I promise you. Go wait outside.'

And with that, they left. I could hear him, moving around the room. I could smell incense burning. A deep lavender scent filled my nostrils. It made me feel at ease. Then I felt his palms press into my back.

'Do not be afraid, child. Do you believe in God?'

'Yes,' I whispered.

He began a slow, melodic chant, and something came over me. He intoned a prayer, and to this day I feel it's the closest to God I have ever been.

I felt my arms and legs grow stronger, almost instantly.

'Now sit in the chair,' he said.

'I can't'.

'Try!'

I closed my eyes and pulled my weary muscles, and for the first time in months they listened to me, and rose on my command. The old man called the others back into the room. They walked in and saw me sitting upright in the chair. Daniel's mother began to cry and she went to hug the old man.

He put his hands out to stop her, and smiled and nodded his head.

'She looks a lot better now, doesn't she?'

I can't explain it. For me, it was a miracle. Some people believe in them, and some people don't. It's hard not to believe when your life is saved.

After three days, I felt better than I had in months. As the weeks and months passed, I became stronger each day. I will never know if it really was the healer who cured me, but I believe it was. I still thank God for that miracle. I had a new lease of life. People say that – a new lease of life – but that is how it felt, like I had signed an agreement for a new life.

Simon came and dropped Roger off at my house. I was so happy to see him. I had my little boy back. I was still very weak but at least we were together. Having Roger there made me feel like things were getting back to normal. I was just so thankful to be alive.

A week later, Simon came to check in and see how I was coping. Roger could barely contain his excitement when he saw his grandfather come through the door. I knew it must be hard for him, having only me for company all day, when I wasn't yet strong enough to play with him or to talk the way we used to. He would be five years old soon, and he was full of energy.

We ate lunch at the kitchen table and Simon told us of all the developments on the farm – a new calf was born the day before. He told us about how he helped the cow to give birth in the middle of the night. Mother and baby were well, he told us, and the calf was finding his feet already. Roger listened intently and I promised him we would go to visit the calf soon.

'What noise does a calf make?' Simon asked Roger, raising his eyebrows. 'Is it quack quack?'

'No!!' Roger laughed with his whole body.

'Is it baaa?' Another burst of laughter.

'It's moooooo, grandad!!'

'Are you sure?'

'Moooooooooooo.'

Roger sat in his grandfather's lap, and Simon talked as Roger clapped his hands against his grandfather's hands. I looked over at the two of them together, and the difference between the two hands – one small and soft, the other big and weathered from hard work, covered in welts and traces of dirt from the farm. I knew those hands so well, and yet they looked older all of a sudden. Maybe it was just seeing them next to Roger's – the next generation of hands.

Simon hugged Roger and raised him high into the air to say goodbye. He gave him a kiss on the forehead, and promised him he could name the newborn calf next time he was at the farm. Roger was delighted.

I walked Simon to the door. It was getting late, and he had a drive ahead of him to get back to Malexander. We said our goodbyes, and just as he was about to leave, he turned around and looked at me, standing in the hallway. He didn't say anything, he just looked. It wasn't like him to be still like that. I looked back at him. Age had taken his colour away – his hair was wispy white and even though he was still a big man in stature, he was a little softer around the edges now, a little less tall. He had wrinkles around his eyes and his eyebrows had grown wild. But he still had colour in his cheeks – those rosy cheeks and the smile I had loved my whole life. He smiled that smile, looked at me for a moment longer, then turned, and left. It's only now I know what he was doing. He was taking it all in, one last time, seeing the little girl who used to follow him around the farm, who used to rest her head on his shoulder by the fire, who always fit, just perfectly, on the handlebar of his bicycle.

It can't have been more than three hours later when I woke to the sound of the telephone ringing. It was Valborg.

'I need you to come,' she said. 'He's dead.'

Just like that she said it. It was like a dagger to my heart. I didn't want to believe it, not until I saw him with my own eyes. He had been fine just a few hours before – so full of life.

Tears rolled down my cheeks. I wiped them away, and gathered my things. It was dark in the house, and I went to wake Roger. I went to his bed and nudged him awake.

'Come on, darling, wake up,' I whispered.

His face contorted, he stretched out his legs and opened his eyes. Moonlight was streaming through his bedroom window. Everything was a hazy blue. He looked confused. Even in the dark he could tell something was wrong. He began to cry.

'Hush, love.'

I patted his back and held him close, knowing his wailing would set me off too.

'We have to go to Malexander,' I said, fetching shoes for him to wear, and kneeling by the bed to put them on his feet.

'Grandad!' he said, drying up his tears.

That made it so much harder.

I sat down on the bed next to him and put my arm around him.

'Your grandad's dead, love. He died tonight when he went home.'

As soon as I said it I wished I could take the words back. It was too quick and harsh for such a young child. To my surprise he knew what the word meant – dead. I picked him up and grabbed my car keys. The tears trickled down his face. I tried to rock him on my shoulder, hushing him. I went to the kitchen, opened the freezer and took out some ice cream. For the whole journey he sat in the back seat, occasionally licking his ice cream. It must have tasted salty with all the tears mixed in with it. It broke my heart to see him like that – his eyes red from tears with ice cream all over him.

I saw the light was on in Simon's room. The stones underneath the tyres made the familiar crunching sound as we drove in.

I had travelled this journey hundreds of times, but I knew it would never be the same again. I parked the car and lifted Roger out of the back seat, trying to wipe away the ice cream from his face with a cloth. We went inside. The kitchen was cold. The fire had gone out. Valborg came into the room, looking tired.

'He's in there,' she said.

I handed Roger to her, and went into Simon's bedroom.

He was lying across the bed, motionless. His face was white. His trademark red cheeks were drained of colour. I ran to him and put my fingers against his neck to check his pulse. Nothing. He was still wearing the clothes I had seen him in, just a few hours earlier. I don't know if that was where he fell ill, or if Valborg had somehow managed to lift him onto the bed. His legs were hanging to one side.

I straightened his legs on the bed, so that he was lying comfortably. Then I burst out crying, knowing it didn't matter anymore whether his body was comfortable or not. He was gone, and he wasn't coming back. I sat on the chair beside him and took his hand. It was cold. It was limp and lifeless. I held it in mine.

I thought of all the times we spent together. I thought about riding through the fields on his bicycle, about visiting Grandma Anna, and most of all I thought about his smile. I tried to soak up the conversations we had had – tried desperately to remember his words, but none were coming. I dropped his hand, stood up and leaned against the wardrobe, breathing fast and loud. I could feel my head getting light, and pins and needles in my legs and hands. I closed my eyes, and tried with all my might not to faint. I waited until my breathing started to slow. I was shocked at what I did next.

'How could you do this!' I found myself shouting. I dropped down to my knees, and beat my fist against the bed.

'How could you leave us? How could you leave me?'

I sat there on the floor, wailing. His heart had exploded, and he was gone from the world. I couldn't believe I would never hear him laugh again.

I walked back into the kitchen. Valborg was sitting at the table with Roger. She had made him some porridge and he was blowing on the spoon of hot oatmeal. I thought of him, a few hours earlier, so happy on his grandfather's lap, and I felt the anger rise in me again. Roger was without a loving grandfather. Now all he would know was the coldness of Valborg.

She looked distracted.

'What happened?' I asked, staring at her as though it was her fault, as though she had neglected him.

I felt that if I had been there, it wouldn't have happened. I wouldn't have let it. But she never minded his heart. She didn't treasure it the way I did.

She spoke, matter-of-factly.

'He went to his bedroom to change, as he always does,

and a few minutes later, I heard a cry. I ran to the room, and he was lying on the ground, clutching his chest, and by the time I knelt beside him, he was gone. It all happened very quickly.'

You could have run faster, I thought. You should have seen the signs. You should have stopped him from being in pain. As I sat across from her, I remembered something she had done to me, when I was only a child. I was ten years old. I had been playing out in the field, and came indoors when she called me for dinner. I sat at the kitchen table, the very table we were sitting at now, to eat. At that moment she had looked over at me, in disgust, and said, 'Why are you so ugly, Kari? What made you so ugly?'

I never forgot how that made me feel. I never felt so unwanted as I did in that moment. I couldn't eat. I just sat there, in shock. I never forgot it. But I had put it to the back of my mind, so that we could live side by side. Now, as I sat there, in that same chair, at that same table, as Simon lay dead in the next room, the truce was up.

I put Roger to bed and tucked him in. My body was still weak and he felt heavy in my arms. I wasn't strong enough for this right now, I thought.

It soon became apparent that the reason Valborg called me to tell me about Simon was not out of duty to me or so that I could pay my respects to my father, but rather so that I would make the funeral arrangements. She didn't seem to care much which relatives knew, or how the ceremony would be conducted. She just wanted him in the ground, and didn't want to know about it. At least that's how it seemed. Maybe that's not fair to her. But that is how I felt during those terrible days.

I wondered if she and Simon ever loved one another, or if it was simply a marriage of convenience. The day after he died, I sat in the kitchen going through old photographs, trying to choose one for the coffin. I noticed that in every photograph of Simon and Valborg there was a space between them. A space the size of me, I thought. At least I loved him, and could fill that gap. No wonder he wanted a child so badly. That day at the orphanage, he saved me. But as I sat looking at the photographs of the two of us, I knew that in a way, I saved him too. I filled that gap in his life, in his heart.

The funeral came. I felt like part of me was buried in the ground that day too. It was the hardest day of my life. As the dirt fell on the coffin lid, I thought I would scream.

The world was a frightening place without Simon. Before him there was nothing, and now, I felt, there would be nothing again. I was weak with fatigue, and weaker still from trying to make all the arrangements. Family came from all over. He was well loved. I took comfort in the number of people gathered at the graveside. I looked up to the sky, and I hoped to God he knew that he was loved.

10

Saying goodbye

A few days after the funeral I left the farm. I couldn't be there without Simon. But being back in Linköping didn't feel right either. I was still angry and tired. I found it hard to sleep at night. I wasn't eating properly. I lost track of the days, and time just seemed to pass.

At first friends came and went, but weeks turned to months and no one knew how to make me feel better, so eventually, they stopped coming. The apartment was a mess. I couldn't bring myself to do the things I had always done – the mothering things that had been so natural to me. The world became a dark place. I had never seen the world like this before. There had always been light, even in the darkest times. But now, everything was grey. I couldn't see a way out. I felt lost. Hopeless. I had fallen into a deep depression and I was still weak from my illness. I wasn't able to cope.

And that's when the worst thing happened. Roger was put into foster care. Just until I was strong enough to look after him again, they told me. There was nowhere else for him to go. Valborg couldn't look after him on her own. And I was sick.

It nearly killed me to see him go, but I knew I couldn't be the person I wanted to be for him, not right then. I kept thinking about the promise I had made to him: to never let him go. But I knew I had to do what was best for him. I had to put him first. As I watched him leave that day I felt my heart breaking all over again. After everything we had come through, how could this be happening?

I was angry with myself after that. I felt like I was Åse. I had abandoned my baby. People got sick everywhere in the world and they kept going, kept being mothers and fathers. People lost loved ones everywhere in the world and they kept going, so why couldn't I?

I felt like I'd let him down, Roger. And Simon.

I stayed in bed all day. I didn't see the point in getting up. I kept wondering what Roger was doing, and most of all, if he was happy. I prayed every night that I would get strong enough to see him again.

It must have been frightening for him, too. But he was in a good place. At least I knew that. He was cared for by a couple who fostered children outside of town. They were very loving to him, and for the first time in his life, he had siblings. Nearly two years passed before I was well enough to bring him home. They were the hardest two years of my life but I was determined to get better for his sake. For Roger's sake. It took a long time, but finally, with help, I was strong again.

And then the day came. Part of me felt guilty for taking him away from his new home, from the brothers and sisters he had grown to love. But I needed him back in my life. He was my son. He cried leaving the house. He didn't want to say goodbye. I was a stranger to him now. For me, it was a wonderful day. I was finally reunited with my son again. My family. But for him, it was like he was being kidnapped from his life for the second time.

It took a long time before he would trust me again, before he remembered me fully, before he felt safe. I could tell he was confused by all the change – by the coming and going, by the loss of his grandfather, and now the loss of his foster family. He was very quiet. Not the laughing child I'd known before. It felt like he was waiting for me to disappoint him again. I felt like I was keeping him hostage. I knew that if he was old enough to walk out the door and make his way back to his foster family, he would have done just that. I was holding him against his will.

He was a little man now, seven. Not the baby I had left two years before. I had missed so much growing up. I tried not to let myself think about it. I tried to pick up where we left off. I wanted to pretend it had never happened – to pretend he had never gone away. Pretend I had never let him go. I reminded him of the things we used to do together. I talked about his father, and how we used to roll his pram down to the park, and feed the ducks, and how he always loved Norrköping, and how I would bring him there again one day. I was trying to reclaim his past.

One night as I was tucking him into bed, he told me that he missed his grandad.

'Me too, love. Me too.'

I sat beside him and took his head in my lap, and combed my fingers through his hair, and told him about the bicycle journeys I took with Simon, and about Simon's mother Anna, and about where he scored the goal on the football pitch, and I told him he reminded me of his grandfather, and that one day he would do all those things too, that there was so much life ahead of him, and that I was very, very proud of him. I think I was trying to convince myself about the future as much as I was trying to convince him.

I could feel a tear roll down my cheek as I pulled him close to me. He tightened his grip around me, and I knew I had my son back. We had both lost our fathers, our pillars of strength, but we had to be strong for each other.

'It's just me and you now, kiddo,' I whispered, 'but it's going to be fine. I'll look after you.'

11

A little romance

The years wore on, and we managed well, the two of us. I took it in steps, and tried to focus on the everyday things, the little miracles that get you from one day to the next, and slowly I began to feel at peace with myself. I was starting to feel like Kari again.

Roger enrolled in a school near the apartment, and I got a new job, in the health centre at SAAB – the Swedish defence and aerospace company. I was tired of hospitals. I'd had enough, having been a patient myself. The smells reminded me of being ill. I was better now and I didn't want to go back to that place in my mind.

When Roger was ten I could see the impact school was having on him. He loved learning. He was a good student. Not at all like me. He must have taken after his father. I helped him with his homework every night, even though I was no good at mathematics. I made him do that by himself. It always put me in a bad mood, when he asked me to help with maths. It reminded me of Daniel, of his notebooks and his beautiful mind. It reminded me that he wasn't there. That he would never help our son with his homework. I felt like we had deprived Roger of a father. Daniel would have been able to show Roger what was good about school. I had always been rebellious in school. I felt the teachers didn't like me, so I fought with them. But Daniel had never experienced that.

Often, sitting at the kitchen table with Roger while he was doing his homework, my mind would drift back to my own schooldays.

I remembered that on my first day we were just getting settled into our new classroom when I heard two teachers speaking to one another, over my head, as if I wasn't there.

'Well, where do you think this bastard child is from? Is she Finnish or what?'

I could feel my face go red. I didn't know why they would see me differently. For the rest of the day I was disobedient. At break time, when the bell sounded, I climbed to the top of the goal posts on the football pitch. The teacher on duty called to me to come down. But I wouldn't. I clung to the post defiantly, goading her, until eventually she gave up. She went back inside and left me on my own, sitting on top of the goalpost, while the classes went on.

I stayed up there for hours. It became a battle of wills. I stayed until the school bell rang, and everyone else had gone home. But I couldn't get those words out of my head.

That evening when I was at home I turned to Simon and said, 'Simon, am I Finnish?'

'What are you talking about?' He looked shocked. 'Where did you get that idea?'

I told him what the teachers had said – that they spoke over my head, and called me 'bastard' and asked if I was Finnish. He was furious. He telephoned the teacher and I could hear him yelling down the line. It was never to happen again, he told her. I had never seen Simon angry before. Afterwards, he paced around the kitchen and talked about home-schooling. He wanted to take me out of the school. I could see that this horrified Valborg – the thought of me at home with them, all the time. She tried to calm him, and said it was in my best interest to stay in school, that he wouldn't be able to manage the farm, and teaching. After a while he seemed convinced. I was disappointed. I loved the idea of staying on the farm. I hated school from that day on.

It was remembering this that made me think about where my life had taken me. I thought about Sven Stolpe, about how he said that I was smart. I had been trying to make myself better, over the past few years, and I knew I had it in me to be something more than I was.

'Mama – what's the capital of Norway?' Roger asked, bringing me back from my daydream.

'Oslo, love.'

He was doing his geography homework. Oslo. I knew where that was alright. I watched Roger, moving his finger across a world map. I found Roger inspiring. I knew it was supposed to be the other way around, but he was so full of curiosity. The way people should be. I made the decision, then and there, that I would go back to school and finish my education. I had left early, at the age of 14, because I could. But I knew better now. I wanted to learn.

I enrolled in adult education classes, and every evening Roger and I sat at the kitchen table, doing our sums together. He loved that Mama had homework too. It gave us something to do together, something we had in common. And it made it easier for me, knowing he enjoyed that time together. I struggled through maths, and just scraped through the exams, and came out with my certificate. The day I got my results I felt I had really achieved something. I was smart, after all. I did it for Simon – to get one up on those teachers who called me a Finnish bastard. He would have loved that. It was about much more than that though. I felt like I could hold my head up high, once I had a certificate. It was only a piece of paper, but it marked the end of a tough few years. It showed we had been strong enough to weather the storm, our little family, and now we were looking to the future, Roger and I.

I had to take the day off work to go to my graduation. So, one of the bosses caught wind that I had graduated, and the news seemed to come at just the right time. The next day he came to the door of the health centre at the factory and asked for me.

'Is Kari here?' he said.

'Yes, that's me.'

'I'm Ulrik Abramsson. I work upstairs in the administration office.'

'Nice to meet you,' I said.

'One of our secretaries has just left, and I was wondering if you might be interested in the position?'

'Me?'

'It's our busiest time of year, and we really do need someone to start straight away. I heard you had been studying recently. I need someone who's good at writing letters and such.'

It took me a moment to process what he was saying. It had all come out of nowhere.

'Eh …'

'Look, if you're not interested, it's fine. Maybe you want to stay working in the health centre. Secretaries are well looked after though, in my office, I can assure you.'

He looked at his watch.

'I'll take it!' I said.

'Great. I'll work it out with management so that you're moved to our department. Would tomorrow be okay to start?'

And just like that I became a secretary for the SAAB company. It was a better-paid job and it meant I was home earlier, to pick Roger up from school and make dinner in the evening.

I had to learn quickly and on my feet. He was right, it was the busiest time, and there was no room for playing catch-up. I liked that though. It focused me. I felt useful again.

It was a much more social type of work, too. The secretaries mingled with the bosses, and we were invited to dinner parties. It had all come at such a good time. I finally felt like being around people again. The social life at SAAB was like nothing I had ever experienced before. They held wonderful parties, with people from all over the world. They were sophisticated, and best of all, there were lots of other single people. I didn't feel like the odd one out, as I had started to feel at times. And that's when I met Claes.

I had noticed him first when I went to collect the invoices from the workshop downstairs. He was fixing an aeroplane engine. He looked over in my direction as my heels clicked across the workshop floor. He was wearing a t-shirt, carrying a wrench in one hand, and there were traces of oil on his biceps. He had long dark hair to his shoulders, and there was a shadow of stubble across his chin. He smiled at me, and winked as I walked the length of the workshop, to the offices at the back. I could feel myself blush. I kept walking, not knowing how to react. I wasn't used to such attention. I was a mother, for goodness' sake. I liked it though. It made me feel young again. Attractive. Wanted. Over the following days, I seemed to find excuses to visit the workshop offices more often. And that's how our romance began.

Claes was different from anyone I had been with before. He was rugged and manly. He was quiet, an introvert, but there was something about him that I was drawn to. He had an inner calm, like he was writing his own story, and nothing could fluster him. The sex made me feel alive again. It had been so long since I'd felt a man's body against mine.

We didn't tell anyone in work that we were seeing one another. It made it more fun – it was our secret. At one dinner party we sat opposite one another, and between glasses of wine, we exchanged glances. He moved his leg against mine, unbeknownst to the other guests. I moved my foot against his thigh and ran my fingers through my hair, trying to contain myself. I could see him, trying hard to focus on the conversation, trying not to give the game away. One conversation was happening above the table, a different one below.

It was exciting. I felt like a woman again. One morning Britt, who sat next to me in work, remarked on the change in me.

'Kari, you seem different,' she said. 'Anything you want to tell me?'

I wondered if they all knew. They must have. I don't think we were as good at hiding as we thought we were.

But it wasn't to last long. Claes was younger than me. He was at a different stage of life. I knew that, but being with him made me feel younger, like it was all still to play for, like I wasn't a divorcee.

But it was just a fling. I knew it couldn't last, so I ended it. It had started to peter out: fewer calls, fewer meaningful glances. I think it had run its course, and I knew I didn't love him. To save both of us the embarrassment, I told him I needed to spend more time with my son, that this arrangement wasn't working out, and I had to put Roger first.

Even though it wasn't love, Claes was something special. He was my bridge, between Daniel and whatever lay ahead. I'll always be grateful to him for that. But breaking up with Claes somehow made me miss Daniel more. It brought it all back. Those early days in Linköping. I felt like I had betrayed him. So many years had passed, and I had tried to put Daniel out of my mind, but he was my first love. Being with Claes just reminded me what it felt like – romance. I tried to remember what Daniel's mother had said to me, about finding love again.

I felt silly, mourning the end of a relationship, a fling, at my age. Like I was a teenager. I wasn't old by any stretch – I was only in my thirties, edging towards forty. Still young at heart. But responsibility has a way of ageing you. The responsibility of parenthood. I tried to get a sense of perspective again. I was glad to have more time to be with Roger, and I couldn't help feeling guilty, like I hadn't been giving him my full attention. I decided I would try to teach him a life lesson – it's what mothers were supposed to do, after all. Simon had always been teaching me lessons, in subtle ways, but the message always got through. He had the knack of pretending everything was a game.

Roger and I had fallen into a routine – the morning wake-up call, breakfast and the rush to school, studies at the kitchen table in the evening, and walks in the park on the weekends. I had been so engrossed in my own life, in my own love life, that I had forgotten Roger needed adventure too.

So that Sunday, instead of sitting at home as we normally did, we got dressed up, and I told him I had a surprise for him.

'A surprise?' His eyes were big as he buttoned his coat and went to grab an umbrella. He was getting so tall. He was nearly 12 now. Soon he would be too old to hang out with Mama. I wanted to make use of the time we had, while he was still my little boy.

We headed out the door and walked a few blocks and turned left. Roger stopped in the middle of the pavement.

'But the park is that way. We always go to the park on Sunday.'

'We do, but we don't have to, Roger. There's something I want to show you.'

There was a travelling church in town. They had pitched a tent in a field in the next suburb. When we arrived, a woman outside the tent greeted us and shook my hand. 'Welcome,' she said.

She had long grey hair to her waist. She was wearing a grey cardigan and a long patchwork skirt. She reminded me of my grandmother.

'And who might you be?' she said, smiling at Roger.

'Roger.'

He looked down at his feet. He could be shy with strangers.

'Well, I hope you enjoy it! Head on in.'

What looked outside to be an ordinary tent was completely different inside. A velvet carpet ran the length of the aisle, and the place was packed with men and women dressed in brightly coloured robes, swaying from side to side, singing gospel music, and clapping their hands.

Roger looked up at me in disbelief.

'What is this?' He seemed excited by the rhythms and the a cappella singing.

'Church,' I said, as we found a space in a pew.

I don't know what made me think of church as the surprise. Perhaps I was feeling I'd lost my way a little, with Claes, and all the goings-on.

After the ceremony, we were walking home and Roger asked me why we went to that church instead of our church.

'Because I want you to know that there are different kinds of churches, and different kinds of people, and that you can choose anything you want in life.'

Roger looked to be taking this in. His brow furrowed in the way that it always did when he was mulling things over. Then a bright green frog jumped across the pavement, and the moment was gone. He ran after it, and crouched down to get a closer look. He beckoned me to come and see. 'Mama, a frog! Look at the colour of it!'

To this day I don't know which left more of an impression on him – the frog or the church service. I was glad we went, though. I knew what it was like to grow up feeling different, and I knew that he was different too, and I worried that somehow the other children would find out. He had never lived anywhere but Sweden. He spoke Swedish and looked Swedish, but he was Norwegian too, and German, an outsider, like me. I just hadn't told him yet.

I nearly told him that day, about his grandmother Åse, but then I decided it wasn't yet time. He wasn't old enough. He had been through enough. He needed time to enjoy his childhood, without more complications, I decided. But some day, he would need to know the truth. Just not that day.

12

We meet again – Oslo, 1986

After our first meeting in 1965, Åse wrote some letters to me. They were mainly filled with small talk. She would tell me about the weather, and sometimes she would mention Per – when she got word of how he was doing. She always sounded very proud of him, even though they lived apart. It was difficult reading about Per when I knew I couldn't reach out to him. It reminded me of that time we spent together, Åse and I.

I often wondered why Åse was going to the trouble to write, when the letters said so little. It was almost like she was trying to remind me that she was still out there. She always ended the letters the same way – Your mother, Åse.

That was all I really had of my mother – that sign-off on a few pieces of paper – a dash and three words. And over the years I read so much meaning into those three words.

In the space of 20 years she sent six letters. It kept her as a presence in my life. But I was a mother now too, I had been busy looking after Roger all those years, and I had left Åse in the past. Or so I thought.

When I was 42, I found myself back in Oslo again. I was on holiday, visiting an old friend. I had thought about contacting Åse before I left Sweden to let her know I was coming, but then I thought better of it. I was just going to enjoy the holiday. No complications.

But perhaps, somewhere deep down, I was ready to revisit my past. I just wasn't admitting it. I had booked a flight to Norway. I hadn't been there since my last visit to Åse. Roger was grown now. Maybe it was time for me to make peace with that part of my life, once and for all.

When I arrived in Oslo, everything about the city – the colour of the buildings, the street signs, the Norwegian lilt – everything – reminded me of that first journey to meet my mother. I tried to put her out of my mind, but every time I saw a woman her age my head turned. I was constantly expecting to bump into her. I saw her in every elderly woman's face. I heard her voice in every stranger's conversation. Sometimes, in a shop or on a street corner, I found myself rehearsing the conversation I would have with her, if I happened to bump into her.

I thought I had put it all behind me, but being there brought it all back. The feelings were so strong I knew I had to do something to put it to rest, for my sanity's sake. I found a phone booth. There was a phonebook inside. I took out one of her letters from my handbag, to find the address, and leafed through the pages of the phonebook until I found her listing. There she was – Åse Løwe. I dialled the number and, after a few rings, she answered.

'Hello.'

'Hello … Åse?' I didn't know what to call her. 'It's Kari here. I'm in Oslo.'

Silence.

I wondered for a moment if she remembered me. She had to. I was being silly.

'I was hoping I might come and visit you.'

I heard her open her mouth to speak. She paused. 'Yes.' She paused again.

I thought she wanted me to give an explanation as to why I was in Norway, when she spoke again. 'You have the new address?'

'I have it here – in your letter,' I said.

'Alright.'

I had forgotten how short she could be. But perhaps I had startled her, I thought. She was getting older, and maybe she was just shocked to hear from me after all this time. I was always giving her the benefit of the doubt.

'Kari …'

'Yes,' I said, thinking she was about to say something about how she felt.

'The afternoons are better for me.'

'I can make it there this afternoon.' I hung up the phone, and stepped back out into the crisp Norwegian air.

I found a bench nearby and sat down, to get over the shock. She always had a way of winding me. I thought about cancelling. She had been frosty over the phone. I thought of those letters. The words seemed so meaningless now.

Suddenly I felt cold, and far away from anything that I knew. I wanted to hug Roger. I still hadn't told him about Åse. He was nearly a man now, he was 17.

I thought about when he was younger, playing in his grandparents' house in Malexander. Malexander – I couldn't think of it as home anymore, now that Simon was no longer there. I imagined the house was cold now and the rooms were empty without him.

I thought of the night I told Roger that his grandfather had died, and how I watched him cry. I thought of how he played with Valborg after Simon passed away. He always brought out the softer side of her, the side I had never seen. He was accepting, forgiving. And then I thought of the worst day, when Roger was taken away from me, and of how my heart broke when I said goodbye to him. But Roger had forgiven me. He had given me another chance.

I had thought of my mother over the years, never sure whether to contact her. In the end I always decided not to. But I was younger then. In your youth, things are often black and white. I was older now. I was a mother myself, and I knew how hard it could be to raise a child, and that sometimes you had to make tough choices for the sake of the child.

So here I was, back in Norway. Somehow life had brought me back again. There was a lot of water under the bridge, and I couldn't help but feel that perhaps I was the one abandoning Åse now. Perhaps I had been too hard on her. Maybe she too had made difficult decisions all those years ago, for my sake.

There was another thing to consider. I wanted my mother to know Roger. And I wanted him to know where he came from. I knew that if she would let me bring him into her life, she would grow to love him. He would bring out the softer side of her, too. Maybe then I would see the softer side of my mother, and maybe then I might grow to love her.

I knew what I had to do. I had to see her again.

So I started to walk in the direction of the city centre, resolute in my decision. I would go and meet my mother again, for Roger's sake, and for mine. Since Simon's death, the longing to know about my past felt even stronger. I think part of me hoped she could fill the hole he left in my heart. I longed to feel protected again.

I took the bus to Åse's new address. It brought back memories of that first meeting. This time the door didn't open on its own. I knocked, and stood back. I felt vulnerable, like the first time I had been to see her. Somehow she still held a power over me. That unnerved me. I didn't let anyone else in my life do that to me, so why should I let her?

I took a deep breath. I didn't know what to expect. But I kept an open mind. This time would be different. We would talk more, woman to woman. I still had a question I wanted to ask her. *Why* she had given me away? Or why was I *taken* from her, as she had told me the last time we met? And how did she feel about it?

I knocked again, a little louder this time. The door opened, and there she was – Åse. I tried not to look surprised. She was much older than I remembered. Twenty years had passed, but she had stayed frozen in time in my mind, and I know it doesn't make sense but I expected her to be as she had been when I first met her. She looked tired, worn down by time.

'Come in,' she said. She didn't smile.

'Welcome,' she muttered as she led me down the corridor towards the kitchen. It was small, just about big enough for two. She motioned for me to sit down. I pulled out a chair, and sat at the table. She sat opposite me. I looked at her. She looked away. She wasn't pleased to see me.

I cleared my throat.

'I'm just in Oslo for a few days ... so I thought I would get in touch. How have you been?'

She brought her index finger to her eye and rubbed it.

'I'm just fine, Kari. Would you like coffee?'

'No. Thank you.'

She was asking because that was what she was supposed to do. It all felt strange and awkward. The conversation was stilted, the pauses were long.

I tried again.

'I got your letters ...'

I thought about those words as I looked at her, marrying the face with the signature – Your mother, Åse. I couldn't imagine her sitting in that same kitchen, at the table, writing those words, and then posting the letters, to me. But she had done that. She must care, I thought. And yet, here I was, sitting right in front of her, her own flesh and blood, and she couldn't even speak to me. For a moment I wondered if she had heard me.

'Kari, I think we should leave it there.'

I felt my pulse race.

'Yes, okay. Maybe I should come again, tomorrow maybe, when you're a little more ...'

'We've met each other now. We've done that.'

She didn't look at me while she spoke. Instead she buried her face in her hands, like she was exasperated. Like I was asking for something unreasonable.

'Let's just leave it in the past now. Let's leave it there,' she said, glancing up for a moment to catch my eye. I didn't know what to say.

What could I say? 'Yes, that's ...' I trailed off. There were no words.

We sat in silence for a minute.

Then finally she said, 'It looks very cold outside.'

'I better go,' I said, standing up from the table and making my way to the door. I couldn't understand how she had slipped so easily from her rejection of me to talk about the weather. I was feeling embarrassed. Even though I was a woman in my forties, I felt like a child again. I wasn't welcome there, and she had told me as much.

I walked towards the front door and turned the handle. I felt a tap on my shoulder. I looked back at her and saw she had her arms outstretched, as she presented me with two crisp white linen cloths with delicate embroidery. She motioned for me to take them.

'I made one, and your grandmother Anna made the other. Please take them,' she said, placing them in my hands. I looked down at the rolls of linen, and then I looked at her for what I knew would be the last time, and left.

I got back on the bus. It was busier now, noisy with the chatter of commuters making their way in and out of the city centre. Condensation clouded the windows. I rubbed my fist against the pane in a circular motion, so I could see where I was going. I looked out at the city street, at the people making their way home in the rain in the dark. I watched a man helping an old woman across the road, as she leaned against his arm. There's a camaraderie among strangers when the weather turns. People look out for one another, as they make the trek home. That's what I love about living in a cold country, the warmth in people. I could see my reflection in the glass looking back at me. But that was the last thing I wanted. I didn't want to see myself at that moment. I felt unloved.

I looked down at the cloth in my lap, and traced my fingers around the pockets of flowers – poppies and daisies. My consolation prize, I thought. I would never understand Åse, and what that gesture meant, those rolled-up pieces of linen. Perhaps she wanted me to have something to remember her by.

And so, she left me with no choice. That day in 1986, I had to close the door on my past, once and for all.

I decided not to tell Roger about Åse. It was all too embarrassing. And he was better off without all that drama.

That would be the end of it now. Or so I thought. But some things you can't control, and I couldn't control what happened next.

13

A place for the unemployed

They say love happens when you least expect it – that when you stop looking for it, it finds you. Well, that's what happened to me.

After Claes, I decided I was too old for romance.

I got my shot at love, with Daniel, and it was wonderful, and then it was over. I was happy with that. Some people never find love. I was lucky.

Love was something for a different stage of life. When I was a teenager I had many boyfriends. I had always been lucky in love. Boys were drawn to me. And even though my marriage was brief, it was more than a lot of people had in a lifetime.

But sometimes I did wonder what it would be like to have someone in my life. And I thought about it even more when Roger moved out of the house and I found myself alone again, at the age of 49. I don't know where the years went. But they passed, and for the most part they were happy years. Roger was going to university. He had passed his exams, and his teachers told me that he showed great promise, and that he had a bright future ahead of him. Life was just as it should be. We had done well, he and I.

The year was 1993. It was one of those beautiful autumnal days in Linköping. The trees were starting to shed their leaves – brown, crimson and orange. There was a chill in the air. Just enough to remind you that you were alive.

With Roger gone, I had a lot of time on my own. I started going down to the local community centre where they held classes and workshops and social gatherings. It was just me now, just Kari again. I had Valborg of course, but she was never the same after Simon died. Though she was never warm, whatever bit of spark she had in her died with him. I think she wanted to die, when he died. Not out of love, really, but out of lack of purpose. She was in a care home and I visited her at the weekends, but there wasn't ever much to say. We never had much to say, through all the years, Valborg and I. Simon was all we had in common, and he was gone. But still, I went. It was my duty I suppose.

Åse had stopped writing letters to me. They used to come when I'd least expect them. Months would go by, sometimes years, and then another letter would come in the post from Norway. I knew by the stamps, and I grew to recognise her writing on the envelopes. This was my mother – these scraps of paper that travelled across the land to fall inside my letterbox. Then, after our meeting in 1986, the letters stopped. Just as she said, we left it there. No more communication. Sometimes I thought about writing to her, but the thought made me angry at myself, and I would put the pen away again.

I tried sometimes to remember what her hands looked like, what her hair looked like. Sometimes I thought I could remember, but I think the image was a mixture of memory and fantasy. As the years wore on, her smile grew softer, her touch warmer and more meaningful. It was hard to distinguish what was real, and what was what I hoped it had been. Sometimes late at night I took out her old letters and read them, again and again. It wasn't much, but as long as the letters were coming, I knew she was out there, somewhere. When the letters stopped, I wondered if she was still alive.

I was thinking about her that day as I walked through the park, towards the community centre. I thought about the first day we met – how frightening it was, and how awkward. I was daydreaming. I could almost feel myself back there – I could smell the staleness of her apartment. I could feel the tension in the back of my neck. Then I felt rain on my face, and it snapped me back to reality, back to Linköping, back to 1993.

It was starting to rain so I ran to the door of the community centre, to take cover before the rain got heavier. I hurried inside, and shook the raindrops from my coat. I ran my fingers through my hair, and as I was taking my coat off, I heard the receptionist and the centre manager arguing about something. I walked into the main room, so that I could hear what it was about. They were arguing about whether or not to allow unemployed people to use the centre.

'No,' I interrupted, from across the room, before I knew what I was doing. I was taking the side of the receptionist.

'Why in heavens would you do that?' I asked. 'You have plenty of people already using the facility. And we pay a lot. You don't need the unemployed as well.'

'Yes, you do!' a voice piped up from the other side of the room.

A tall, slender man with round glasses stood up from the chair he was sitting on. I hadn't noticed he was there. In his green khaki coat, he had nearly blended in with the green walls of the centre. When he stood he was remarkably tall. We all looked up at him.

'You don't want the likes of me here, is it? I'm unemployed. Would I ruin the centre for you?' He looked at me, in a way that put me in my place. He towered over me. I hadn't thought of someone like him being unemployed. But here in front of me was an educated man, an unemployed man, a handsome man, to whom I now owed an apology.

'I'm sorry ...' I said. 'I never thought ...'

'No, and that's just the thing – you never thought. People don't!'

He looked at me a moment, and then happy in the knowledge that I had been taught a lesson, he softened, and put out his hand. Unsure what to do next, I took his hand in mine.

'Sven Rosvall,' he said.

'Nice to meet you. My name is Kari,' I said, blushing. He smiled.

Over the weeks that followed, we spent time together in the centre, drank tea, and talked for hours on end. We never arranged to meet, but somehow we both showed up each day at around the same time, and acted surprised to see each other.

I was 49 years old. This was to be my fiftieth year on earth – a big one, they say. People talk about getting old, going grey, and getting closer to death, but what they don't talk about is the self-assurance that comes with age. The confidence. Of course you're full of lumps and bumps, and your body's not what it used to be, and you have scars and wrinkles, but you feel more comfortable in your skin as you grow older, strangely more so than in your slim, lean, short-skirt days. I felt like myself around this man. We made each other laugh.

And as the weeks and months passed, we formed a friendship I had never known before in all my years. I couldn't believe I had reached this stage of my life without meeting him. We would talk for hours. We argued and debated. He challenged me. He had a way of looking at life. His company had gone bust. He had lost his job, but he was optimistic about the future – always looking forward. He made me see the good in things. I had a lot of hurt that I needed to talk through. I didn't know that until I met him.

He asked me 'why' a lot, and 'how' – why I did things and how I felt about them. No one had ever cared enough to ask before. I was just Kari. I got on with things, at least on the surface. He really wanted to know what was beneath the surface.

Our friendship grew, and from friendship we found love, and passion. He was younger than me, by nearly 15 years, closer to Roger's age in fact, or somewhere in between. And he knew Roger. They had studied together on a course. I wondered if it wasn't a little strange, to be friendly with my son's acquaintance, but as we got to know each other, I no longer had a choice. There was a strong connection there, and it had formed, and couldn't be undone. Roger was a little awkward at first when I told him about Sven. 'Sven Rosvall?' he asked, one evening when he was home for a visit. He looked surprised.

'Yes, I think you've met him,' I said cautiously.

'Isn't he a little young for you?'

'Maybe ...' I said. 'We're just good friends.'

I was fooling no one. But as the months passed, Roger spent time with us, and the idea seemed to grow on him. He was just being protective after all. For so long, it had just been him and me. It was difficult for him to imagine me as anything other than his mother. And then one day, he gave us his blessing.

'I think you're good together. Very cute,' he teased. And that settled things.

I was always grateful to my son for that. He knew I needed someone in my life, now that he was gone, and when he saw us together, the way we laughed, it all made sense. This was our new family. I knew I was in love with Sven, and I needed to be with him. The more we saw each other, the more I wanted to see of him.

My fiftieth birthday was approaching. I was embarrassed to tell Sven, as it just reminded us both of the age difference. But of course, he knew. He was only 35. Fifty was a long way off for him. I hadn't thought much about how to celebrate. 'Some dinner maybe,' I suggested when

Sven asked. 'Nothing fancy though. Just a nice night. Just the two of us.'

I woke up late on the day of my birthday and pottered around the kitchen making myself a late breakfast. I was planning a quiet day in, and a dinner at our favourite restaurant in the evening.

Little did I know that Roger had other ideas. There was a knock at the door. I turned the latch and was immediately taken aback.

Three of my closest friends, who I had met in adult education classes, were standing on the doorstep. 'SURPRISE!' they yelled. 'HAPPY BIRTHDAY!!'

'Oh my goodness!' I said. 'What are you all doing here? This is a wonderful surprise!'

'Oh, just wait … there's more!' said Eva-Britt.

'Get dressed, Kari!' said Ingrid, barging past me into the house. 'You've got to get dressed quickly!' She looked at her watch. 'There isn't much time to spare!'

'What's going on?' I asked, disorientated by all the noise and commotion that had suddenly taken over the house. It all seemed so frantic.

'Hurry! We're going to be late!' she said.

'Okay, okay.' I ran upstairs to my bedroom to find something to wear.

'Wear trousers!' yelled Ingrid from downstairs.

'Well, that settles that question!' I thought, and hurried into a blouse and a pair of jeans.

Everything went quiet. I poked my head around the bedroom door to see if they were still downstairs. The front door was open. I heard the car doors slam closed, followed by a beeping of the horn. I grabbed my house keys and hurried out the door, wondering what on earth this could be about.

I clambered into the back-seat with Eva-Britt. They all looked around at me. I was flustered from having gotten dressed so quickly.

'Well …' said Berit, 'are you excited?'

I laughed. 'I haven't a clue what to think!'

Eva-Britt leaned into her handbag and produced a long silk cloth. 'Ta da!' she said.

'What's that?' I said, laughing nervously.

'Kari,' Ingrid explained, pointing to the cloth, 'you'll have to put this blindfold on, so it's a surprise to the very end.'

Eva-Britt covered my eyes with the cloth and tied a knot at the back of my head.

'Too tight or is it okay?' she asked, with her hands on my shoulders.

'It's fine!' I said. 'I feel like I'm being kidnapped!'

They laughed. The car trundled along. It felt like we were driving for the longest time. I was starting to feel claustrophobic. I could feel every bump in the road. I reached for the handle to wind the window down and felt a cold blast of air hitting my face.

'Are we nearly there?' I asked.

'Almost!' said Eva-Britt, suddenly coming to life.

A few minutes later the car stopped.

'Here we are!' said Ingrid as I heard the car doors open, and shut.

'I'll come and help you out, Kari! Leave the blindfold on!' said Eva-Britt.

The car door opened and I got out, as Eva-Britt held my hand.

'That's it! I've got you!' she said.

I stepped forward, slowly and carefully finding my footing. Eva-Britt was very slight. I didn't think she would be able to catch me if I fell. I could hear the crunching of gravel beneath my shoes.

Eva-Britt put her arm around me and led me a few steps forward. 'Ready?'

I could smell petrol in the air and could just make out the low hum of a Cessna engine. From all my time at SAAB I can tell a plane's engine a mile away. 'I think so!' I said, anxious for the big reveal. Ingrid took the blindfold off. I blinked my eyes to get used to the light and tried to focus in front of me. We were on the tarmac at a small provincial airport, and in front of me was a banner, with capital letters, which spelled out the words 'PARACHUTE JUMPING'.

'Oh my God!' I squealed, looking around to the others, my mouth open in disbelief.

'Happy birthday, Kari!'

At that moment a man in a jumpsuit came out of the shed, and smiled over at us.

'You must be Kari!' he said. 'I'm Erik. What a surprise for you. What birthday is this? Or is it rude to ask a lady?' He turned to the others, with a flirtatious wink.

'Behave!' said Berit. 'We're in trouble … you're a man in uniform!'

'I'm in shock!' I said, putting my hand over my mouth.

'Well, not too much time for that,' said Erik, laughing. 'Time to get kitted out! You're up next!'

We boarded the plane and took off. We climbed higher and higher into the sky. It was the most alive I had ever felt. The engines were roaring, the plane door was wide open. All I could see for miles around was the Swedish countryside.

'Are you nervous?' asked Erik.

'Not at all! I'm ready!' I said, and I really meant it.

'Alright, remember what I told you? FIVE … FOUR … THREE … TWO … ONE!'

I felt my foot leave the metal ledge, and all of a sudden I was falling through the air. The world beneath me was getting closer and closer. Erik tugged on the strap, and the parachute opened and we began to glide. Everything slowed, and I looked around, floating in the clouds, high above the world. It was magical. I asked him if it was possible to see Malexander from where we were.

He pointed and I could just about make out, far in the distance, the lakes and forests of Malexander as we glided back down to earth.

I was on a high for the rest of the day. It was a wonderful birthday present. Everyone had chipped in, but it was all Roger's idea. He knew I'd love it. And it made me feel loved. We had talked about it once before, years ago, when we drove past an airport advertising parachute jumping. I found out afterwards that Sven had refused to play a part in it. He didn't want to be involved and tried to pretend it wasn't happening. He couldn't rest easy until he knew I had landed safely back on earth. It frightened him to think that something might happen to me. I understood that. I would be the same about him. That's when I knew he truly cared.

It made it an easy decision when he asked me if I would move to Ireland with him. I took out an atlas, and looked at Ireland on the map – a little island on the western edge of Europe. It would be a big change. Sven had been offered a job in Ireland with Microsoft and he wanted me to go with him. I agreed immediately.

'Let's go!' I said.

And a few weeks later, we had packed up our lives and said goodbye to Sweden. I was ready for a new chapter in life.

14

Ireland, 1997

'The last stop before America,' said Sven as we boarded the plane. I laughed. This was going to be an adventure, I could feel it. There was nothing keeping me in Sweden any longer. Roger was leading his own life and was very busy with work, Valborg had passed away, and I was ready for something new. Sven's job sounded promising, and Ireland's economy was on the rise. It was an island full of opportunities.

Dublin became our new home. We knew it was a big step, but we didn't know yet if we were quite ready for all the steps we were about to take. Or at least he didn't.

'What about marriage?' I asked Sven one night as we were eating dinner.

He took a sip from his wine. 'Let's see how things go, Kari. It might be too much too soon. Let's just see how we get on.'

I agreed we should be pragmatic about the relationship. We were both adults, and we had both done a lot of living before we met each other. We weren't naïve about love. We wanted to test the waters first, before we took the plunge.

I suppose the age difference was a factor. We hadn't known each other for very long – just four years – and we were in a new country, away from friends and family, and everything that was familiar to us. It was going to be the ultimate test.

So we lived together in Dublin, and made a home for ourselves. As the months went by we grew more comfortable in one another's company and it just felt right. We knew very quickly that our relationship passed the test. We were good together, anywhere.

It was Saint Valentine's Day, 1998, when Sven asked me to marry him. I was fetching groceries to make dinner for the two of us. I headed back through the shortcut, as I always did. But when I turned the corner by the green, I noticed something unusual. Sven's car was in the driveway. He was supposed to be in work. I walked a little faster, hoping there was nothing wrong.

I stopped in the driveway. Sven was standing in the doorframe, just looking out at me. He must have seen me coming up the street.

'Sven,' I said. I walked towards him. 'Is everything okay?'

Then I noticed the way he was looking at me. I could feel that something was going on. I walked up to the door. I opened my mouth to speak. Sven put his finger to my lips.

'Kari,' he said, 'can you tell me why you love me?'

I looked at him and smiled. 'Because you're kind,

you're caring, you're funny, we have a lot in common ...'
I could have gone on, but Sven interrupted.

'Kari, will you marry me?'

'Yes!' I said, and we hugged and kissed right there in the doorway, for all the neighbourhood to see. It was a movie moment. The shopping bag fell to my feet. I held him in my arms, and I never wanted to let him go.

'How did I get to be so lucky, to find a man like you?' I said, looking into his eyes.

'It's me that's lucky,' he said.

'So, where to get married?' Sven asked the next morning as we planted geraniums together and weeded the garden. Back to wonderful normality. That was the only question that remained – where.

'What about the community centre?'

Sven laughed, and nodded. 'It makes sense!'

A few weeks later we flew back to Sweden. We didn't want a fuss, just a small ceremony with close friends and family. I wished Simon could have been there, but I knew he would be smiling down on us.

They decorated the community centre, with colourful bunting hanging from the ceiling.

The hall was decked out with two sets of seats on either side of the room, making an aisle. Everything was ready. Friends and family arrived. Music played. And then came the most important moment.

'Do you, Sven, take Kari ...?'

'I do.'

'Do you, Kari ...?'

'I do.'

The only known picture of myself as a baby, which I didn't see until I entered the seventh decade of my life.

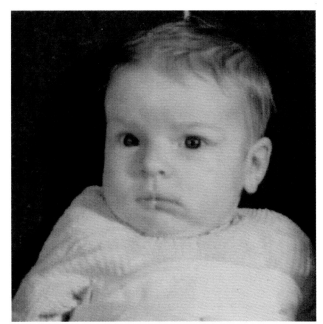

At ten days old, I was packed in a crate along with other Lebensborn babies and sent from Norway to Germany, where I arrived at a Lebensborn home, such as the one pictured here, called Hohehorst, in northwestern Germany.

I was one year old when the war ended, and I was a refugee – the result of a doomed project – with no place in the world. My name is underlined on this passenger list of refugee children taken from Germany to an orphanage in Sweden.

liggare	namnet			ligg.		
∠ 7 894	Wagman, E. ica	Tj		1	1	j	f.41
∠ 7 895	Gross, Renee	Tj		1	1	j	f.33
∠ 7 896	Gross, Herta	Tj		1	1	j	f.35
∠ 7 897	Holländer, Egon	Tj	1		1	j	f.39
∠ 7898	Klein, Otto	Jugo	1		1	j	f.34
∠ 7 899	Klein, Albert	Jugo	1		1	j	f.36
∠ 7 900	Weiss, Eva	Tj		1	1	j	f.32
2 7 901	Friedmann, Olga	Ung		1	1	j	f.32
∠ 7 902	Fischer, Elvira	Rum		1	1	j	f.33
∠ 7 903	Klein, Elisabeth	Ung		1	1	j	f.31
∠ 79 04	Katz, Eva	Ung		1	1	j	f.38
∠ 7 905	Rothstein, Lenke	Ung		1	1	j	f.31
∠ 7906	Kallus, Rudolf	Holl	1		1	j	f.35
∠ 7907	Hirsch, Bela	Holl	1		1	j	f.31
∠ 7 908	Schwarz, Eveline	Tysk	1	1	1	j	f.40
∠ 790 9	Kranzova, Hermina	Tj		1	1	j	
∠ 7 910	Gertzek, Luba (Kryszynska)	Pol		1	1		j	
2 79 21	Dworakowski, Stanislaw	Pol	1		1		
∠ 7 922	Marcinkowski, Stefan	Pol	1		1		
∠ 79 23	Malak, Boleslaw	Pol	1		1		
∠ 7737	Svanevit, Fritz	Norsk	1		1		f.43
∠ 7738	Olsen, Tordism Gudmund	Norsk	1		1		f.44
∠ 7739	Petersen Jan	Norsk	1		1		f.43
∠ 7740	Löwe, Kari	Norsk		1	1		f.44
∠ 7741	Guldbransen, Erik	Norsk	1		1		f.43
∠ 7742	alderhau, Turi	Norsk		1	1		f.43
∠ 7743	Nygaard, Karl Sigfrid	Norsk	1		1		f.43
∠ 7744	Arnesen, Heinz	Norsk	1		1		f.43
∠ 7745	Johansen Klaus Dieter	Norsk	1		1		f.43
		Norsk	1		1		f.44
	tz	Norsk	1		1		f.44
		Norsk	1		1		f.44
		Norsk	1		1		f.44

Simon and Valborg, my Swedish parents, who adopted me at age three.

I had a happy childhood, nurtured by the love of my adoring father, Simon. But not all the family accepted me, and from the time I knew of my adoption, I longed o know the story of my origins. It would be many decades before it fully emerged.

On a school trip with classmates and teacher.

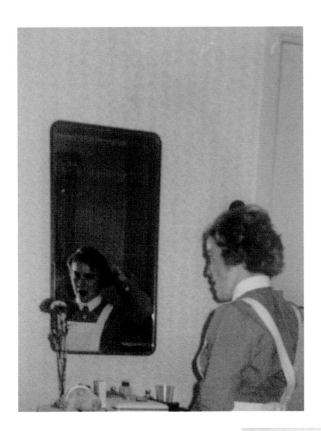

It was during my time as an auxiliary nurse that I began the search to find my birth mother. I waited in anticipation for weeks after I contacted the Red Cross, until finally word arrived...

Åse Løwe, my birth mother, as a young woman in Norway.

My adoptive Swedish father Simon and I had a special bond, and when he died, my world fell apart.

My beloved son Roger, whom I raised alone, has always been my pride and joy. Here he is as a young man in uniform.

Meeting Sven, my second husband, brought me great happiness. Together we came to Ireland, where we have found a true home.

Discovering the truth of my begininngs when I was in my sixties came as a shock – but it was also as if the missing piece of the jigsaw had finally been found. This is the official Norwegian record of my parents. I never found my father.

I / 5 4 3 1

KV: Z e i d l e r, Kurt. Feldp.Nr.
geb:

KM: L ö w e, Aase. Wohnort: Larvik.
geb: 6.10.1917

Kind: Entb:

When I visited Hohehorst, now home to a small museum, I had no memory of my time there as a child. Yet I was haunted by the thought that it was here I had been consigned to an attic, motherless, at the outset of my life. It was heart-breaking – but I was thankful that, somehow, I had survived.

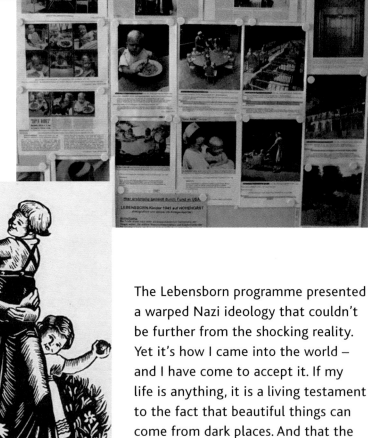

The Lebensborn programme presented a warped Nazi ideology that couldn't be further from the shocking reality. Yet it's how I came into the world – and I have come to accept it. If my life is anything, it is a living testament to the fact that beautiful things can come from dark places. And that the light of love always shines through.

As a young girl, I played with my imaginary brother Peter in the country fields of my Swedish home, where I was raised as an only child. I could never have imagined that I had an actual half-brother, Per, in Norway. We did not find each other until much later in life. Now these two photos of us as small children take pride of place, side by side, on my mantelpiece.

Although I would always love my mother, our relationship would never be straightforward. Sadly, Åse bore too many scars from the war. In her way, though, she was a strong woman, and I recognise part of that strength in myself.

One of the high points of my life was visiting President Mary McAleese at Áras an Uachtaráin, with the Irish Scandinavian Club. She knew nothing of my origins but her simple question touched my heart: 'Are the Irish kind to you?' And the resounding answer was, 'Yes.' In Ireland, I finally found a place called home.

Today, with the love of my life, Sven.

It was perfect.

The celebrations were wonderful. Confetti flew through the air. We ate cake and drank champagne and danced late into the night.

'It's hard to believe,' Sven said, when we found a quiet moment together at the table.

'I know,' I said. 'Just think, five years ago, we first shook hands here.'

'And here we are now. The Rosvalls!'

It's funny, the places life takes you.

When we returned to Ireland after the ceremony, members of the Swedish community, our friends and neighbours hosted a dinner party to celebrate our marriage. We popped champagne and I felt young again and, more importantly, I felt at home. I had never known that sensation before. I had never felt safe, protected, like someone else would care for me if things went wrong. I caught Sven's eye in the midst of all the merriment, and I knew this was meant to be. All the noise drowned out when we looked at each other. Like it was just him and me, Kari and Sven. I was the happiest I had ever been.

It was an exciting time, nesting like young lovebirds, and creating a whole new life for ourselves.

One day, we went to a furniture store to buy a new couch and we seemed to be causing a bit of a commotion in the store. People were looking over at us.

Finally, a teenager came over in his shop uniform.

'Can I help you?' he asked awkwardly, looking towards the security guard at the exit.

We were laid out on one of the couches together in the middle of the showroom.

'We have to make sure it's good for kissing on,' we told him.

He looked at us for a moment, and hurried off, in apparent disgust. We laughed. We were in love. People think that's only for the young. That's how it's advertised. But it's there for everyone.

We still make each other laugh. It's the only ingredient really, when all is said and done. I loved that time. I felt like I was starting over, reinvented in a different land, until the past reared its head again.

'They want a copy of your birth certificate,' Sven said, sifting through the paperwork. We were buying a house, and were trying to finalise everything with the bank.

'Do they really need one?'

'Looks like it.'

'Well, that's too bad,' I said. 'I don't have one.'

I was tired of coming up against this problem every time I tried to process any official document in life.

'Yeah, I know. Is there anything though? Anything we could give them?'

'There's really nothing.'

All my life, I was asked the question, 'Where were you born?' I never really knew what to say but I usually got around it, until some authority figure asked for an answer in writing.

Most people ticked the box, but for me it was always a problem. I knew I was born in Norway, because Åse told me so, but I had nothing to prove it.

'I'm sure we'll be able to work something out,' Sven said.

'You can't escape your past,' I said. 'Especially if you don't have one.'

Sven looked sorry he'd brought up the topic. It wasn't fair that I played that card.

'Sorry, I shouldn't have brought it up. I know there's no birth cert. But there must be some way around it.'

And sure enough, we did find a way around it and we bought our house, in Dundrum, a quiet suburb in south Dublin. When we had been to view the house first the neighbours asked us in for tea. That's when I knew we had to live there. This was the right place for us.

We spent months painting the walls and taking up the carpets. The house was a little bit of Ireland and a little bit of Sweden. We started a blog, to tell people back home about how we were adjusting to life in a new country. The Irish accent was the hardest thing to get used to. It's difficult for a Swedish ear, we wrote on the blog. The voices are so full of enthusiasm, but it can be hard to make out the words. It makes it tough sometimes to know when to laugh, in case you misjudge the joke. But we were laughing a lot, nonetheless. And we soon got used to the Dublin accent, and considered ourselves expert, until we ventured further from Dublin, and had to contend with the more rural varieties. Then we knew we had a little more to learn.

We loved taking it all in. We visited all kinds of places around Ireland. And we were keen to keep meeting new people. Sven even joined a motorcycling club. He loves his motorbike. One day he came home and showed me a list, with 24 place names on it.

'It's a task they set all the members,' he told me. 'I have to visit them all!'

He had to journey to every place on the list, by motorbike, and take a photograph to prove that he was there. Sven accepted the challenge and began mapping out his routes.

Every weekend he kissed me goodbye, and jumped on his motorbike to explore somewhere new. I joined the Irish Countrywomen's Association – it was a group of Irish women who met every week to make crafts, or go to talks or go on trips together.

And Sven and I took lots of holidays together – visiting friends in South America and exploring European cities. If only Sven Stolpe could see me now, I thought! I was a long way from Malexander.

We were enjoying life. And we even started to live by what we termed 'Irish time'. Over the years we relaxed into the rhythms of the place. It was all about people, not punctuality.

So, in Ireland it was always acceptable to be late. In fact, you were expected to be. It took us a while to learn that. In the beginning, when we were invited to someone's house for eight o'clock, we showed up at eight o'clock, much to the horror of our hosts. We soon learned eight is code for eight-thirty – at the earliest.

But we learned all these things as we went on, and the years flew by.

And before we knew it, nearly ten years had passed and we seemed to have become more Irish than the Irish. We weren't blow-ins anymore. We were locals.

And so, when we were invited to a dinner party one night with the Irish Scandinavian Club, we found ourselves wondering which clock to go by – Irish time or Swedish time. We settled for something in between – eight-fifteen. Little did I know that this party would change the rest of my life. And to think I almost didn't go.

15

Björn

It was a cold winter's evening.

'Kari!' Sven called from the car.

He was running the engine so that the ice on the windscreen would defrost.

I was rummaging through the wardrobe, trying to find my gloves.

'Kari, we're late!'

'Coming!'

When we arrived at our friends' house they made a fuss and fetched us wine. A log fire burned in an open grate, making the room warm and cosy. We were glad to be in from the cold. While we were waiting for dinner to be served, the guests mingled in the living room. There were a few unfamiliar faces at the gathering. That's what was nice about the Irish Scandinavian Club, it connected everyone, and you were always meeting new people.

I was deep in conversation with one of the other Swedish women, when she turned to introduce me to a friend of hers who was standing on his own.

'Kari, have you met Björn?' she said, bringing him into the conversation.

'Hello. Where are you from?' he asked.

'Dundrum.'

'No, I mean, where are you *really* from?'

I wanted to say Dundrum again, but instead I said, 'Sweden.'

I thought it was what he wanted to hear.

'Kari doesn't sound Swedish. Where in Sweden were you born?'

'Well … I wasn't actually born in Sweden.'

'Where, then?'

'Norway.'

'I love Norway. I often go there in the summer. What part?'

'Oslo.'

'Ah, lovely. So what brought you to Sweden?' He tossed a handful of peanuts into his mouth.

'Well … I grew up there.' So many questions.

'Your parents moved there?'

'No,' I said. A small group of people were looking at me now. 'I was adopted,' I said. 'My biological mother is from Norway.' I leaned over the coffee table to take a handful of crisps, hoping that was the end of the conversation.

I felt a hand on my shoulder. Björn again.

'Kari, I know this is strange, but do you mind me asking what year you were born?'

It was like an inquisition.

'This is funny. I have yet to hear a single thing about you! Only that your name is Björn.'

'I know ... I'm sorry. I'm just ... interested.'

'1944. But I thought you were never supposed to ask a lady her age.'

'Don't worry, we're all friends here. And, tell me, how much do you know about your mother?'

It was getting a bit personal now. People normally don't pry when you say you're adopted. They assume the worst and just move on from the topic.

'Well ... not a lot, I suppose. Only that she's Norwegian.'

'And your father?'

'I never met him. He was German.'

'German?'

'Yes.'

'That sounds about right ...'

'What do you mean?'

He looked like he wasn't sure whether or not to say what he was thinking. He took another handful of nuts.

I was curious now. 'What is it?' I said.

'Well ... I'm not sure how to say this to you ... Actually, no. Never mind.'

'You really have me wondering now, Björn.'

'Well, would you mind if I had a look into your family history?'

I took another sip of wine.

'It might be nothing, but I just want to check something.'

'How do you mean?' I asked.

'1944, you said?'

'Yes.'

'And your mother's name was?'

'Åse. Åse Løwe.'

'Okay, I'll be in touch,' he said, and moved over to the other side of the room.

I was left there, dumbfounded, not knowing what had just happened. Sven appeared beside me and put his arm across my shoulder.

'Everything okay?' he whispered.

'Yeah, fine,' I said. 'I think.'

All through dinner, I found myself watching Björn, trying to figure him out. He seemed normal, not the eccentric I might have suspected him to be. Hugely intelligent, from what I could gather. He was the historian for the Irish Scandinavian Club, and seemed to be very knowledgeable about both Irish and Scandinavian history. At least that might explain his interest in my family history. Still, it was all very peculiar.

That night as we drove home I told Sven about our conversation. I wanted to know if he thought it strange.

'No, I'd say it's probably something he just does for the society. I think he's been appointed the historian or something. I wouldn't worry. The dessert was lovely though, wasn't it?'

So we thought no more of Björn, until the following Monday. I was sitting at the computer in the study, writing an email to Roger, when a pop-up at the bottom of the screen said, 'New email message from Björn'. I clicked on the link, and up came the email.

Hello, Kari. It was lovely to meet you the other night at the Irish Scandinavian dinner. I have been doing some research into your family history. I might have something that would be of interest to you.

Let me know if you have time to go for a coffee soon
and we can discuss it.

Kind regards,

Björn.

I closed the email and wondered what on earth he could
mean by that. I didn't really like people knowing my business.

I went back to my email to Roger. My son was now
working with the Japanese embassy in Stockholm, and
was on a business trip to Tokyo. His email to me had
been sent 20 minutes before, and I was hoping to catch
him while he was still online, to let him know we were
thinking about him.

I sent the email to Roger, and looked up at the clock on
the wall: 5.35 pm. Sven would be home soon. I hurried
downstairs and began slicing potatoes for a potato gratin.
A few minutes later the door swung open and in walked
Sven, slightly out of breath.

'I took advantage of the nice weather, and cycled,' he
said, kissing me on the cheek as he made his way through
to the living room. He threw his bags down and collapsed
on the couch. 'Ahhh,' he said. 'That's better.'

I finished making dinner, and we both sat down to
eat. Sven looked tired. It was a busy day at the office.
His position at work meant he had a lot of responsibility
and the pressure was always on. He was good at his job
though, and took it in his stride. He didn't let it get the
better of him. I always found that very attractive in a man.
It was reassuring.

He told me that he had managed to pick up some of the pieces we needed for the model railway we were building. After dinner we moved into the sitting room. We sat there, silently, enjoying the evening, painting the train parts of the model that distinctive Swedish red, when I suddenly remembered the email.

'What do you think?' I asked, after I had recited the email to Sven.

'I'd say meet up with him.'

He was fond of Björn. They had talked a lot at the dinner party. Sven was also a keen historian, and I could see he appreciated Björn's intellect and curiosity.

'At least hear what he has to say,' Sven said, carefully adding a coat of black paint to the miniature engine parts.

'Maybe he just wants help with the society history archives, and is trying to get you onside. Who knows? No harm in meeting for a coffee.'

The next morning, I replied to Björn's email. I invited him to come to the house over the weekend.

So, that Saturday I was in the back garden with Sven when we heard a knock on the door.

'Door's open!' Sven yelled. 'We're out the back!'

Björn followed the sound of our voices to the garden, and stood in the doorway, admiring our work.

'Quite the gardeners!' he said.

'It's coming along nicely,' I said, taking off my gardening gloves, and sticking the trowel into the earth for safe-keeping.

We brushed off our hands and shoes and headed back into the kitchen.

'Let's have some tea and biscuits!' I said, and put the kettle on.

Once we were all sitting around the table, Björn started things off.

'So, Kari … I feel I need to explain my behaviour the other night. You see, I had a feeling about you, and I think I might be right.'

'Go on,' said Sven, coming to my aid.

'Well, this is going to come as quite a shock, and bear in mind, I could be wrong about this …'

'What is it, Björn?' I asked, suddenly nervous about what he might say next.

'Well, a group from Norway was in touch with us recently. They've reached out to Scandinavian societies all over, about a court case that they're involved in, and they want anyone who might be affected to be aware of the fact.'

'A court case?'

'Yes, Kari, but no need to worry.' He could see I was getting anxious.

Sven and I looked at one another.

'Björn, I think you better come out and just say it. We can handle it. Whatever it is. Kari's been through a lot in her life.'

Björn looked at me.

'I think there is a possibility that you may have been one of the Lebensborn babies.'

He left it hanging in the air.

'What does that mean?'

'Well, obviously, I can't know for sure …'

'Yes, but what is it – Le-bens-born?'

'Well … How do I explain this …? During the Second World War the Germans, well, the Nazis, wanted to create a "super race" by breeding blonde-haired, blue-eyed children, so they chose women with Aryan features to have babies with SS officers. These officers were an elite corps fanatically loyal to Adolf Hitler and the Nazi party … and … I don't know how to put this …'

'Go on,' said Sven.

'Well, many of those women were Norwegian … and the babies were sent to Sweden, after the war. It might explain your name, and your adoption, and move to Sweden. And your German father.'

'SS officers? Nazis?' It all sounded like something from a different world.

Sweden had been relatively unaffected by the war, so I had never thought much about it.

'Yes, I'm afraid so. It was a programme under the auspices of Heinrich Himmler. I've been reading some of the work of a Norwegian historian by the name of Lars Borgersrud. I can put you in touch with him if you like. I think he would know more than I can find out from here. And as I say, I might be way off the mark, but we've been told to alert anyone who might have been through this programme, as there is a group of Lebensborn children who are taking a case to seek compensation. I just thought you should be aware.'

'It just all sounds … far-fetched,' I said.

'I know, and as I say, it may be nothing. Please don't feel

you even have to look into it. We can just leave it there. We never have to talk about it again if you don't want to.'

The thought of dragging up the past again, getting my mother involved, seemed exhausting.

'Let's just leave it,' said Björn. 'I'm sorry I brought it up. It wasn't my place.'

'No, I'm curious,' I said, surprising even myself. 'I want to know everything there is to know about this.'

'Okay,' said Björn. 'I'll help whatever way I can.'

'But I have tried to find out information about my past before. It's ... not easy,' I said.

'Well, here's the name of the historian who might be able to help.' He scribbled a name and email address on a scrap of paper. 'It's a start anyway.'

We thanked Björn for coming and waved him goodbye. It wasn't until the door was shut behind him that I really began to process what he had said.

'Lebensborn.' I couldn't grasp what that meant. He had talked about SS officers. I thought of the words my mother had said about my father: 'He was not a nice man.' All I knew was that he was German. But for some reason, I had never thought, even for a moment, that he might have been a Nazi, an elite SS officer. I couldn't sleep that night, tossing and turning. I woke Sven without meaning to.

'Are you alright, Kari?' he whispered.

'Yes ... it's just hard to sleep.'

'Try not to think about it if you can. There's nothing to say it has anything to do with you.'

'Yeah, you're right. It's just ... what if ...?'

16

Digging

The following day I wrote to Lars Borgersrud, the historian Björn had said might be able to tell me more about the Lebensborn programme. I asked him if he could help me to find out if any of what Björn had said applied to me. I gave him what little details I had – that my mother, Åse Løwe, had given birth to me in Oslo in 1944, that my father was German, but I didn't know anything else about him, and that I was later adopted by a Swedish family, at three years of age. What happened in these three dark years, nobody knew. I stopped typing mid-sentence.

This was ridiculous, I thought. I was writing to a stranger, giving him my life story, to ask him things I had no idea about. I started deleting the words in the email, and then I stopped again. I tried to think of all the reasons that it couldn't be true. But a lot of what Björn said did seem to add up. What if it *was* true? I was adopted, and I had a Norwegian mother and a German father. It seemed to match what he said about the programme. It might explain how I had ended up in the orphanage in Sweden. It was a possibility. And ever since Björn said those awful words – 'Lebensborn', 'SS', 'Nazi' – they were all I could think of. I needed to put my mind at ease – to know for sure that none of it had anything to do with me. I sent the email.

The next morning I woke early. I heard the front door open and close as Sven left for work. I went to the study and checked my emails. I had three new messages.

One was from Roger with the subject line 'Greetings from Tokyo'; another was from my friend in Linköping – 'Hello, Kari'; and the third was from Björn – 'Yesterday'. Nothing from the historian.

I opened the email from Björn, hoping it would shed some light on what he had said. The email merely thanked us for having him to the house, and wished me luck with my search. He apologised for the way in which he had explained the whole thing. He hoped it hadn't been too presumptuous but said that if I ever needed to talk about it further, he would be happy to help. I decided to try and put it out of my mind until I heard back from Lars Borgersrud.

I went downstairs to work on the greeting cards I was making to sell at the Irish Countrywomen's Association craft market. I found crafts therapeutic. The cutting and gluing and sewing usually helped to take my mind off things. But it wasn't working this time. My mind was still fixated on the conversation with Björn.

'Lebensborn', 'SS', 'Nazi'. Those were strong words.

They were foreign concepts to me but they kept going

through my head. I went back through everything my mother and I had talked about, searching for clues. But Åse was meticulous when it came to keeping secrets. There was nothing in anything she said. I had a headache so I decided to go back to bed. I went upstairs and got under the duvet, and fell into a deep sleep.

The next thing I heard was the front door open and close again. I had slept the whole day through. I heard Sven climbing the stairs, calling my name. He sounded concerned. It was very unlike me not to be in the house when he got home. I heard his steps coming closer, and the door to the bedroom open.

'Are you alright?'

'I just couldn't sleep last night. I came in here to have a short lie down and I must have drifted off.'

'Are you hungry? I'm going to make some dinner,' he said.

'Yes,' I said, still half asleep, and turned back over.

When I woke again, Sven was trying to manoeuvre the door with his elbow, while carrying a tray.

'Dinner in bed,' he said, and presented me with the tray.

I sat up and made a space on my lap on top of the duvet.

'Thank you, Sven,' I said. 'What a lovely surprise.'

'How are you feeling?' he asked.

'I'll be fine. Just tired. It's just all a bit confusing.'

'I know. But we don't know anything yet. It might all be about nothing.'

It came three days later, when I had finally stopped watching my inbox. An email from Lars Borgersrud.

I clicked on the link to open it. I felt nervous. At the beginning of the email, before he said anything else, he thanked me for writing to him, and apologised for not writing back sooner.

He said that he would post me a copy of his thesis, and he would highlight the chapter which might relate to me. It might be a start, he said, but he was sorry he couldn't tell me any more about my family. I responded straight away with my postal address and thanked him for his help.

By the end of the week, the documents arrived in the post. I flicked through the pages of the text, desperately searching for the part he had highlighted. I found it and read the section again and again. The dates matched perfectly. A group of Norwegian children, babies, taken to Germany as part of the Lebensborn, and then transferred to Sweden.

Lars Borgersrud's paper explained what the Lebensborn was – just as Björn had said. The Nazis' attempt to create a 'master race'. To breed children. And some of the children were from Norway.

I looked at the photographs – swastikas and rows and rows of people giving the 'Heil Hitler' salute. I telephoned Sven and asked him to come home early, if he could. He had meetings, but said he would be home as soon as he could get away. Lars Borgersrud's documents suggested there was archive material kept by the Norwegian and Swedish governments that listed the names of the children involved.

I was in a panic. I telephoned the office of the Norwegian archives to demand that any papers pertaining to me should be released. I needed to know if I was part of this picture, and if my mother was. But most of all, I wanted to know about my father. I told myself there was no real proof of anything. But I still felt very uneasy.

They put me on hold. They gave me other numbers to call, other addresses to write to. By the time I was put through to the fifth person, I could feel a lump forming in my throat. I felt closer to the truth than I had ever been, and yet, these papers which might have my name on them, which might hold the answers to all of my questions, were locked away somewhere, and no one wanted to let me see them. This is how I felt, at least. By the time Sven came in the door, I was sitting in the study, on the floor, with all the papers spread out around me.

'What's happened?' he said.

And I told him.

17

The photograph

The next few weeks were difficult. I felt agitated all the time. I seemed to spend most of my life waiting for answers, waiting for strangers to offer up information about my past.

Then one morning, as I was getting ready to go out to the shops, I heard the postman pushing letters through the letterbox. Sven went to the door, and ran back upstairs to his study.

'There's something for you, Kari, from Norway!'

My heart skipped a beat. For a moment I thought of my mother. She was the only one who ever wrote to me from Norway.

'You open it, Sven,' I called up the stairs. He came to the banister, and looked down at me in the hallway.

'But Kari, it's addressed to you.'

'I can't,' I said, and went into the kitchen.

A moment or two passed before Sven came to the top of the stairs again, and called down to the kitchen, 'Kari, you've got to come. Quick!'

I wondered if Åse was dead.

I walked into the study, and Sven turned to me. He handed me something.

'Kari, it's you.'

'What? What do you mean it's me?'

It was a photograph of a baby.

'Look at the back.'

I turned it over. And on the back were the words, 'Kari Løwe, born 6th September 1944'.

Sven looked at me and then at the photograph. 'Amazing, isn't it?'

I was 64 years old and had never seen a photograph of myself as a baby before. Sven had albums full of photographs from his childhood. I was used to poring over them, pointing out his dimples, and the little outfits he was put in as a child. But this was different. This was just too strange. Why had someone posted a photograph of me as a baby, when I was in my sixties? Who had sent this, and what did it mean?

For me, this was completely new. I had assumed there were no photographs of me as a baby. The story of my life didn't exist until Simon and Valborg took me from the orphanage to Malexander.

I looked in the envelope. It was full of documents sent by the Norwegian government.

They were archive documents, a letter explained, from the 1930s and 40s which had finally been released by the government. It was difficult to make out at first what the documents were and why they related to me. I thought of that word again – Lebensborn.

Sven leafed through the pages, studying the wording closely while I stared at the photograph.

'Kari,' Sven said, and put his hand on my hand, 'it's true.'

'What?' I asked.

Suddenly the room felt cold.

'It says here that you were a Lebensborn child. And look at this.' He handed me a sheet of paper.

It was a record of my birth and the details of my parents:

Mother: Åse Løwe
Father: Kurt Zeidler

Kurt Zeidler. It was the most German name I had ever seen. This was my father. Kurt Zeidler. The man I had wondered about all my life. The man Åse had kept a secret.

It didn't have any other details about him, just a name.

Sven handed me another document. 'I think you should read this,' he said.

18

The truth

And so it was, that on that day I began to piece together the story of my life, the full story, including those mysterious first years.

What I discovered was nothing short of incredible. It was dark, but at least I finally knew where I came from.

I was a Lebensborn child. That was true. But what did that mean? It was still so foreign to me. The war. The Nazis. The Lebensborn. I had heard the terrible stories of the Holocaust, but I had never heard of this before.

Sven and I talked it over, for hours, for days. We tried to make sense of it. I had never really thought about history much. It didn't interest me. But now I had to try to piece it together in my mind. I had to see how it all related to me, and to Åse.

We researched as much information as we could – any books we could find, and online. We went through everything slowly, carefully. I had to know exactly what this meant.

To understand it all we had to go back as far as the

outbreak of the war, to before I was born, to 1939. On 1 September of that year, Germany invaded Poland – an action which would change the course of millions of lives around the world. Two days later, Britain and France declared war on Germany. And so began a bloody conflict which would take the lives of 60 million people around the world, and affect many others after that.

A year later, in April 1940, the Germans invaded Norway. Åse lived in Norway. She was 23 years old that year. It must have been very frightening. It was one of the darkest times in human history.

And at the centre of it all, in Germany, were two men – Adolf Hitler and Heinrich Himmler.

Hitler was ruthless. His power was based on racist ideology. In his book, called *Mein Kampf*, which means 'My Struggle', he wrote about the Aryan race. He said it was necessary for Germans to 'occupy themselves not merely with the breeding of dogs, horses, and cats but also with care for the purity of their own blood'. He wrote *Mein Kampf* while he was in prison back in 1924. He was angry about Germany's collapse after the First World War in 1918 and he wanted to rise up again. I can imagine him there, in the dark quiet of his cell, writing page upon page in the dead of night. Words of anger and determination which could only come from a man locked behind bars, waiting to seek vengeance on the world. The book would sell millions of copies. It became the Nazi bible. It was those pages and those thoughts, that propaganda, that would help Hitler in his rise to power in 1933. And the Third Reich gained momentum from there.

Heinrich Himmler was second-in-command to Adolf Hitler, and leader of the SS. He was Hitler's henchman. And it was Himmler who was in charge of the Lebensborn.

Obsessed with eugenics, and the idea of the perfect race, Himmler devised the 'Lebensborn programme'. Lebensborn means 'spring of life'. It had begun slowly, secretly, in 1935. It was one of the greatest secrets of Nazi Germany – a breeding programme which encouraged SS men to have children with Aryan women to create a superior race. With the outbreak of war, the Nazi leaders wanted to ensure the future of the Third Reich with strong Aryan blood. And the Lebensborn programme became a bigger part of their plan.

They set up more Lebensborn homes to house the mothers and babies of the programme. Many of the buildings they used were former nursing homes, or houses that had once belonged to wealthy Jews. They promised to provide a safe place for unmarried pregnant women to give birth to children of Nazi soldiers, away from prying eyes and social stigma. At first the homes were only in Germany. There were ten in total. Then, as Germany occupied other countries, Himmler set his sights on Norway. Eventually he would establish nine Lebensborn homes in Norway.

Himmler was sure this scheme would work. He sent out a message to his SS officers telling them to fulfil their 'sacred duty to the Reich' – to father a 'super race'. He said: 'Should we succeed in establishing this Nordic race and from this seedbed produce a race of 200 million, then the world will belong to us.'

So, at the same time that Nazis were killing Jews as part of the Final Solution, they were quietly growing their own population. The SS would provide the genetic seed of the so-called Aryan race. Those same soldiers who were killing people and terrorising them if they didn't fit into the Nazi world view, were impregnating women to create what they believed would be the 'master race' – a future generation in their image.

There were death camps, and breeding camps. I was born in the breeding camp.

A horrible thought struck me. What kind of man could my father had been? What terrible things might he have done?

And then I thought, in a strange way, if I was part of this programme, it meant that Heinrich Himmler was somehow like a father. He created all of us. He was father to all of us – the blonde-haired, blue-eyed babies of the Third Reich. He manufactured us.

I shuddered at the thought.

What did that make me? A product of some kind of experiment? Like something in a laboratory?

Something from Hitler's laboratory.

I read somewhere that Hitler said: 'I do not doubt for a moment, despite certain people's scepticism, that within 100 or so years from now all the German elite will be a product of the SS.' That was the plan. That was *his* plan. The SS men living in Germany would find German women to impregnate; those in the occupied territories, like Norway, needed to find Norwegian women who would fulfil the requirements.

Åse, I thought. My God. Where did she fit into all of this?

From 1940 to 1945 Norway was occupied. So, in all that time, the legitimate Norwegian government was forced into exile, operating from London, and a puppet government took over, under Vidkun Quisling. He collaborated with the occupying forces. It was all far more complicated than that but what is important for this story is that Norway was in the hands of the Germans and this suited Heinrich Himmler, who had a particular interest in the people of Norway, given their Aryan looks. Norwegian people for the most part had fair hair, pale skin, blue eyes, and athletic physiques. They were the Aryan race the Germans aspired to be.

Women who were potential candidates for the programme were tested by doctors, who examined their physique, down to every last detail, measuring even the bridge of their nose. They had to provide a family history, proving that they had 'pure blood', going back three generations. Some women in Germany must have wanted to be part of that Nazi dream for the future, but for others, who were coerced, it must have been like torture. Their futures hung in the balance of that test – to determine whether they would make the grade and would be granted refuge to have some soldier's baby.

Åse must have passed their test. But I couldn't imagine her as part of all of this. What was her role in this Nazi plan?

I tried to imagine the extent of this madness. Was it intended that for every Jew poisoned in a gas chamber, another Aryan child would be born? They must have come at the same moment – the last cry of a Jewish child being burnt to death in a concentration camp, and the first cry of an Aryan baby of the Lebensborn. The Nazis playing God – creating life and extinguishing it, one child in Auschwitz, the other in Norway.

I felt like I could hear the screams – the piercing scream of death, and of first life – and I did not know which was which.

Nearly 12,000 babies in Norway were born into the Lebensborn programme.

I was one of those babies.

I looked at all the documents spread out in front of me – the names of places, the dates.

My name.

My birthday.

This is real, I thought.

This isn't just history. This is me.

I tried to go back there in my mind. To imagine what it was like. Back to wartime. To the day I was born.

I closed my eyes to try and go through the details, slowly – bit by bit. The story of my birth.

I was born in Norway.

Born of a Norwegian woman and a Nazi soldier.

It was 6 September 1944.

The world was at war, for the second time in half a century.

I imagine the scene. I imagine Åse, as she was in Oslo when I visited her. But I know she must have looked younger then, back in 1944.

I can smell the sea nearby, and the antiseptic from the hospital ward. I hear the sound of soldiers passing in the street.

A man approaches the bed, black hair combed back. His skin is pale. He has dark circles under his eyes. He wears round spectacles, and an officer's uniform. On his arms there is a crest, like a spider being sucked into a drain.

Heinrich Himmler is his name. He looks at me – a newborn bundle. He laughs with the nurse.

'This is a good one.' I remind him of his daughter, he says.

'She's a sturdy thing. Strong.'

Åse Løwe, my mother, is sitting on damp white sheets, exhausted from the throes of childbirth. She says nothing. She's done her job; she's given birth. It took 48 hours. She has produced a girl, me, weighing eight pounds, seven ounces, and 52 centimetres long.

I don't know if she feels guilty or sad. I can't imagine her feelings.

She must have cradled me for those ten days. Or maybe she left me to cry in the cot beside her, not wanting to get attached to me.

I drink from her breast. We are connected in that way.

We must have been. She was my mother. And then again, she wasn't.

I don't know. All I have are the documents. And the documents show that after ten days in the hospital with my mother, I was taken away by a nurse.

I imagine she wears a white uniform, like the one I wore as a nurse. I could never take a child away from a mother. How could any nurse do that?

I was then sent to a Lebensborn home near Oslo. Because I had a German father, and a Norwegian mother.

I will never know if my mother agreed to give me away or not. The documents don't say.

My mother never told me.

All I know is that ten days after I was born, she left the hospital without me. And I was in the hands of the Nazis. I was their property.

I think that's where they took the photograph of me. The one that came through my letterbox so many years later.

Sitting at my kitchen table in Dublin, I look down at that photograph of me as a baby. In the photograph, the baby is looking up at the camera. I try to imagine what the baby is looking at – who was on the other side of the lens. A Nazi soldier with a camera, looking down at a baby. Looking down at me. Property of the Reich.

After the photograph was taken they selected the healthiest children. They took us from the home and packed us in boxes. We would travel to Germany. If we lived, we lived. If we died, we would be thrown away, like animals. I was number I/5431.

I know they took us from Oslo to Lübeck, in Germany, but I can only imagine what that journey must have been like. I imagine a man, employed to do a transit job, with a van, packing the children tightly in the back of the vehicle, as if we were vegetables for market, or animals to the slaughter. Each baby lying in a makeshift crib, travelling the road to the sea, while our guardian, the transit man, smoked a cigarette out the car window, trying to ignore the crying babies in his trunk. I imagine the sound of all those babies crying as the van passed over potholes and difficult terrain. He would deliver us, that batch of babies, to people waiting at the dock, to a boat that would take us to Germany.

We were just there to be used. A commodity. I was number I/5431. I survived. I was lucky, in that sense, at least. I passed the test.

Once on German soil we were taken to another Lebensborn home, called Hohehorst, in the north-western part of the country in a place called Bremen. We were to be part of the Aryan race. Blonde-haired and blue-eyed, all products of Nazi men and pure Aryan women. The Nazis decided who would live or die. Decided who would be born, and when. Who would die, and when.

They say the ground in Auschwitz is still full of ash. I could never bring myself to go there. I cannot even go there in my mind.

I have seen the images though, the queues of women and children, naked, not knowing, shuffling into the chamber, waiting to be washed down. And yet, to the Nazis, they were the dark stain on humanity. They were evil, to be obliterated. Innocent children. Innocent people.

It frightens me to think that I was once a part of Himmler's plan. That he was my maker.

I was on my own in the house one afternoon. Sven was at work. Weeks had passed since the documents had arrived in the post. My mind was still full of questions and frightening thoughts.

I took a book from the shelf, about the Second World War. I wanted to find out more about this man – my creator. I flicked through the pages, and found a photograph of Heinrich Himmler. His hair is dark. He looks weak for a man with so much authority. He is at a Nazi gathering. Thousands of men sit in rows behind him, all in uniform. There is a sea of swastikas. It would make you dizzy to see them. On his lap is his daughter, his biological daughter. She has blonde hair. He holds her like a father should, shielding her from the world. She looks safe in his arms. I see myself in her.

I closed the book, and went to the back door for air. As I walked through the hall, I caught my reflection in the mirror above the sink in the bathroom.

I used to see Kari. Now I don't know what I am.

I was bred to be perfect – Aryan – but I know that I am not perfect. I cannot control that. I wonder what they had in mind for me, what they hoped I would become. How they would have used me.

According to the documents, I lived in Hohehorst for the first year of my life. I was at the very heart of the Lebensborn.

My first year on earth, without parents, in the care of an SS programme, under the watchful eye of Heinrich Himmler.

I could read it all there, in the documents that had come through my letterbox.

The house felt like it had been invaded.

I tried to imagine it all. I could see it written down, but I couldn't believe it. Or I didn't want to believe it. It was like they were talking about someone else.

Hohehorst. What was that place? What did it mean to my life?

I needed to see it with my own eyes, to know that it had really happened.

Later, Sven and I talked it over, and we decided that it would be good to retrace my steps, to see where I had been as a child. It might help me to understand. It might bring closure.

So we took out the maps, and made a plan.

'We'll do it together,' Sven said.

I loved him for that.

We booked our plane tickets to Germany. We would take a trip to Hohehorst, to see the Lebensborn house, and to find out what went on there.

I thought back to that night in Linköping years before, when I had written to The Red Cross. I thought of the longing to meet my real parents. I thought of the call to tell me that my parents were German and Norwegian. I thought of all the people I imagined they might be. I could never have imagined this scenario.

I had searched for my past all my life, and now that I had found it, I almost wished I hadn't.

I had travelled to Norway to meet my mother. But I was half-German too. And now I had to face that side of my past as well.

I was just so glad that Sven was with me this time. We would go together. I wasn't in this alone.

19

Hohehorst

A few days later we took off from Dublin airport and landed in Bremen. We rented a car and followed a map to Hohehorst. The journey could have been hard, but it wasn't. Somehow, Sven made it okay for me. He made it normal. To the point where we almost forgot what was bringing us on the journey in the first place. I always feel excited about planes and airports and new places, and Sven and I loved travelling together. We called everything an adventure, and this felt like another adventure.

It was only as we were getting closer to our destination, as the car turned the final corner towards the Hohehorst house, that it dawned on me what we were doing.

There was obviously a reason my mother had kept all this a secret. I didn't know what I was going to see in Hohehorst. Perhaps we should turn back.

I had spent so much of my life trying to block out the bad memories, to keep feelings down. I didn't know what this was going to bring up in me.

'Here we are,' said Sven, as the car came to a stop

outside the Hohehorst house. He looked at me to see my reaction. He turned off the car engine, and we both sat in silence looking at the building in front of us, through thick black iron gates. We got out of the car. The gates were locked. But there was a gate lodge to the left which had a sign in the window. We couldn't quite make out what it said until we got closer – 'Lebensborn Museum'.

Seeing the words was chilling. It made me realise that this thing had made enough of an impact to warrant a museum. And I was a part of that.

As we walked around to the front of the gate lodge, we saw another sign hanging in the doorway – 'Closed Today'. There was a phone number at the bottom in small print and a man's name.

'Let's go, Sven,' I said, walking back towards the car.

I was quietly relieved. Now that I had seen the house and the word 'Lebensborn', I didn't want to see any more of the place. I got to the car door. It was locked. I turned to see if Sven was coming with the keys. He was still at the door of the lodge, pacing, talking on his mobile, speaking in broken German.

He snapped his mobile shut and said, 'It's sorted! He's coming down now to open the museum.'

'What?' I said, finding it difficult to mask my disappointment.

'We've come all this way, Kari. At least give it a chance.'

He told me that when he rang the man to ask about opening hours, the man was reticent at first. He said, 'We're closed today. Maybe come back tomorrow.'

But when Sven told him that his wife was a Lebensborn child, who had lived in Hohehorst and that she was hoping to see the museum, the man changed his tone immediately.

'Wait there,' he said. 'Don't move. I'm coming down!'

Five minutes later, a car rounded the corner at speed, and came to a stop outside the iron gates.

A man in his fifties got out. He looked at me, and shook my hand. He spoke to me in German. I could just about make out what he was saying, though he was speaking quickly. His eyes were wide, and he was gesticulating wildly. He seemed excited to meet me. Sven shook his hand. We were lucky that Sven could speak a little German.

Hans was the man's name. He led us back up towards the cabin, and explained that he had spent many years gathering all of the photographs, and the history of the house, as he hoped for it never to be forgotten. Sven translated for me.

We went inside and suddenly I didn't need a translator anymore. The pictures said it all. The walls were covered with photographs of women and children, and of Nazi soldiers. And because I could not recognise myself as a baby, I saw myself in every photograph. I knew that I must have been in some of them, and so, imagined myself in every frame. It was frightening to see it there, staring back at me. This was the closest thing to a family photograph album I would ever have. And it was on the wall of a museum.

It seemed real now.

In one photograph a group of children were gathered behind a nurse, making the 'Heil Hitler' sign. In another, three cots side by side, next to an open window. I wondered if I had been in one of those cots. The babies in the photograph were asleep under blankets. One of them might have been me.

In another photograph, a man with a Nazi uniform is measuring a woman's face with a ruler – a potential mother for the programme. I shuddered and thought of Åse. To the right of the photograph, another picture showed the delivery room with sharp medical instruments on an operating table.

How clinical the whole programme must have been, I thought. How frightening to give birth like that. I couldn't imagine it. It seemed such a sinister place. And yet, the children in the photographs are smiling and playing with the nurses who are caring for them, with the ominous SS flags flying above. The innocence of childhood – we wouldn't have known what we were a part of.

As I walked around the room, I could feel Hans, our guide, watching me, studying me. His life's work has been to document the lives of these children and babies. He knows their past, and there was I, their future, standing in front of him, appearing as if from nowhere, on a quiet Sunday afternoon.

I get the impression that the purpose of the small museum is to simply show what happened, and acknowledge the pain of the victims, in the hope that somehow this knowledge will ensure it never happens again.

He asked if we would like to see the house. He opened the metal gates, and we made our way towards the ornate building which overlooks the gardens.

It has three floors, and rows of windows across the front. Statues line the verandah. As we got closer to the house I felt numb. Sven translated for me as Hans told us the story of what happened to the children in the house. I was looking at everything around me, trying to absorb it. Trying desperately to remember it.

We reached the house, and as we stood on the portico I looked inside. There seemed to be endless rooms with chandeliers and winding staircases. As I looked in through the window a man's face appeared. I jumped back. Sven laughed and put his arm around me. The man in the window smiled, and waved to signal that he hadn't meant to scare me.

The house was now an addiction centre, Hans told us. He asked if we'd like to go inside. And to this day, I don't know why I didn't go. I don't know if it was the man in the window – the thoughts of interfering with whatever routine was being carried out inside – or if I had come too close to that part of my past. Maybe it was all too much to take in. I had lived with the Nazis. I was embedded, as a baby. I had been one of them, and I worried that being in those rooms might bring me back to that place in my mind.

Sven looked at me. He has always been curious, always wanting to know more about the world. I know if it had been up to him we would have gone inside, but as the three of us stood there on the verandah, there was an unspoken agreement that the decision was mine, and mine alone.

Hans told us how the house had been repaired over the years. He had grown up in the area, hearing stories all his life, about the house and about what used to happen there.

As he recounted the history of the house, he filled in the gaps of my life, of what happened to me after I was taken to Hohehorst.

∼❧∽

In 1944 I arrived in Hohehorst, along with other babies from Norway. We had travelled over sea and land to get there. We were packed side by side in makeshift cots. When we got to the Lebensborn home, there were other children there.

Some had come from Norway, just like me, fresh out of the womb. Others were older – kidnapped from Eastern Europe, because of their Aryan looks.

They would be raised as Germans. Their past was gone, and they would never know where they had come from. All because they had blonde hair. Some say those who proved not to be Aryan enough were sent to the concentration camps. Our fates were decided by the length of our noses, or the colour of our hair.

For those who passed the test, no expense was spared. Hohehorst, our new home, was big and ostentatious. There were granite sculptures, long corridors, high ceilings and sprawling lawns. On sunny days the children would take the air out on the balcony, cared for by ladies in white aprons. They would push us along in prams with wooden wheels.

And there I was, one of the little girls and boys brought over from Norway to be raised by strangers.

A whitewashed fountain stood symbolically near the front entrance, with water cascading down.

It was called the Lebensborn programme – 'fountain of life'. This was the fountain. We were the life. We were Hitler's children, the future leaders of Europe. Aryan. Perfect.

Back then, we lived our days, innocent and ignorant of what was going on around us. We were the chosen ones to be cared for, protected and groomed under the watchful eye of the Nazis.

To think that all this happened to me, to Kari, before Simon and Valborg found me and brought me to Malexander. It feels like a completely different story. Someone else's story. I find it hard to see it as the story of my life.

20

Himmler & Hitler

So many things I cannot know of what went on in this house in Hohehorst. But what frightens me most is that there I swore allegiance to Adolf Hitler. I promised to follow him and to devote my life to him. Even though I was too young to even talk. It chills me to think of this. But it happened, and I can't undo it.

I learned that the Lebensborn children were baptised under the Nazi flag, a welcoming into the inner circle. They held a ceremony. An altar was draped with a cloth, and there was a large swastika overhead. A pillow was placed on the floor before the altar. As a baby, I would have been laid on it. SS soldiers held a dagger over me, in a symbolic gesture, while reading excerpts from *Mein Kampf* aloud. One of the soldiers concluded the ceremony by proclaiming an oath, swearing a lifelong allegiance to Hitler and Nazi ideology on my behalf. And that was it. I was sworn in. I was Kari Løwe. Number I/5431, a child of the SS. One of Hitler's children.

It wasn't a mother and father at my baptism. It wasn't Simon and Valborg. It was soldiers. Nazi soldiers.

I get angry sometimes, about the war, about what it did to my mother, and about what it did to me. I blame Hitler. But without Hitler, there would be no Kari. This makes it harder for me to hate him. But I do. But in hating Hitler, am I also hating myself? These thoughts are the consequences of my unnatural birth.

Adolf Hitler wanted to be an artist. He loved painting. But the art school he applied to rejected him. I wonder if he felt angry about that. I've seen a quote from him, about art, where he says, 'Anyone who sees and paints a sky green and fields blue ought to be sterilised.'

As I looked at the Lebensborn house in front of me, with its sprawling green lawns, I wondered if this was how he saw the perfect picture. This spring of life.

I cannot imagine such a man. And to think that some woman loved him. And he loved Eva Braun. Their love story was a tragic one. They were together for over a decade before he married her, finally, in a bunker in Berlin in April 1945, as they hid from the world like cowards. And their life together ended a few hours later in suicide. They swallowed cyanide and Hitler shot himself in the head. And there he died under the earth. They never had any children, and yet, all of us, the thousands of children of the Lebensborn, were his. We were his creation. His legacy.

Heinrich Himmler also took his own life at the end of the war. But how confused his mind must have been, to believe the things he did. Before he was involved in the Nazi party, he was a chicken farmer. He practised selective breeding, to create pure white chickens. From chickens, he moved on to people. To think, that's how he saw us, like chickens to be bred. Himmler's pure white chickens.

They saw the Third Reich as a Utopia. Fit, healthy people procreating, to make more fit, healthy people. They thought if they could weed out the weak genes, they would be unstoppable, unbreakable.

The Nazis sterilised the disabled and the mentally ill. The footage is frightening. There was a campaign to dehumanise those with illnesses and disabilities, to make them seem unworthy of life. As someone who spent so much time working in hospitals, that idea is alien to me.

It was all part of the promotion of the 'master race'. Women were just fodder for the glory of the Fatherland. The Führer's plan was on course. Eugenics and the Final Solution were working side by side in the service of evil.

Hitler thought his reign would last forever.

And then, one day, the war ended. Everything changed. Hitler was defeated.

He was gone, and we remained. What would become of us – the broken pieces left behind after the war.

21

After the war

As Hans brought us through the history of Hohehorst, Sven and I pieced together the story of my life, matching the dates with those on my documents. I can see the story clearly now, or as clearly as all the bits of the puzzle will allow.

Hans told us what Hohehorst was like in its glory days, in Hitler's glory days, and then what it was like after the Germans were defeated, when everything changed for me and the other children at the house and, in fact, all the children of the Lebensborn.

We had been branded pure blood and perfect, but now we were the outcasts. Nobody and nowhere wanted us.

Hans pointed to the top of the house. He told us that Hohehorst was taken over by foreign soldiers in 1945, the year I was there, when I was just a baby. He said the children of the house were banished to the attic. And as I stood there, looking up at the roof of the house, towards the attic, I could almost feel the itch of lice in my hair. I could smell the stench of all those children, sleeping together, side by side, with no water to bathe in and little room to move for weeks on end.

I tried to imagine the people who had cared for us up in the attic. Those same women in white aprons, their lives turned upside down. They must have been afraid. There must have been soldiers everywhere. The Allied armies pouring into Germany. Hohehorst stood like a monument to a dead regime, once so powerful, now crushed.

We were the leftovers, the babies hiding at the top of the house. I thought: thank goodness I was a baby. We wouldn't have known what was happening. We were in the same house but the world was different. We were so far away from the sprawling gardens and the white fountain where we had once played. The whooshing of the fountain outside was menacing now, taking its regular breaths, between the sounds of gunfire in the dead of night, like it was cheering them on. The world was a frightening place.

We should have been sent back to Norway. But the Norwegians now hated anything to do with the Nazis. We were too much of a reminder of how things were. We would not be safe there. So it was decided we would go somewhere neutral, somewhere we didn't have a history at all. We would be sent to Sweden.

On 23 July 1945 we were rescued by members of The Swedish Red Cross. They came in white vans with red crosses, to take us to safety.

We arrived at an orphanage in Sweden three days later.

We were given new numbers. I was number 7740. The orphanage deloused us with DDT. A few days later, my papers show, I was brought to a clinic to be checked for lung disease. I was still only a baby, not even a year old.

Then, on 23 August, I was moved again, taken to another part of Sweden, to another orphanage, called Fiskeboda. So there I was, a baby with no history, and nowhere to call home. I was nowhere's child. It remained to be seen whether I would find a family, or continue to live in the care of the state.

I had been number I/5431 in Germany.

Now, an orphan in Sweden, I was number 7740.

But I wasn't those things. I was me. I was Kari.

Simon and Valborg were out there somewhere. I didn't know them and they didn't know me. I was a baby with nobody in the world to love me. I would one day be their daughter, but for now I was a refugee, a castaway from an evil regime.

22

The orphanage

The Fiskeboda orphanage was not a good place. The lucky ones found homes. But that's what it all came down to – luck. The people running the orphanage put ads in the local papers, looking for willing couples to take orphaned children.

When people came to the orphanage to adopt a child, we were lined up in a viewing gallery. I was only a baby, so a nurse must have held me in the line. The men and women walked the length of the corridor, inspecting the children, before choosing a child to take home. The rest of us were left there. No homes for us today.

And so it went on. For weeks people came and went and no one chose me. Until one day, on 8 September, a woman, named in the documents simply as 'Mrs Grahs', came to Fiskeboda to look at me, to see if she would adopt me. She must have heard there was a baby up for adoption. I imagine babies were easier to adopt as you could raise them as your own. I must have passed her inspection, as she chose me from the viewing gallery. It must have been my lucky day. And by 23 September, the adoption was granted, and Mr and Mrs Grahs came to collect their new child.

My new parents applied for a passport for me. They wanted me to have Swedish citizenship. I would be Swedish from then on. Everything was set in stone, or so it seemed. Then, six months later, Mrs Grahs's husband died. The man who would have been my father.

I must have been there, at the funeral. A few days later, I was brought back to the orphanage.

Mrs Grahs told the orphanage that her circumstances had changed. She was no longer in a position to raise a child.

The women in the orphanage were not happy to see me. I now cost them money. Children, once adopted, should never be brought back. I think they soon forgot about me, as it wasn't until nearly four months later, on 12 July 1946, that I was sent to a children's hospital for observation. The orphanage had decided they couldn't keep me either.

They wanted to get some kind of certificate to say that I had special needs, and needed to be sent to an institution. This would take me off their hands. The doctors examined me. They found me unresponsive. I hadn't developed any speech, and wasn't reactive enough for an infant my age. A few weeks later, when I was back at the orphanage, the paperwork came through – a note from the doctor, signed by the Department of Health, to say that I was mentally challenged and should be permanently institutionalised. I had lived in two orphanages already, and had been sent back by the parents who had adopted me. Now things were about to get even worse.

They waited for the final documents to come through so that I could be sent to an asylum. The months went by. Other children left the orphanage, while I remained. Some were adopted, some were sent to institutions. Two very different sentences – one meant life, the other was no life at all.

I had been on the waiting list for nearly a year. There were no positions available for me yet. They decided they could no longer care for me in Fiskeboda, so I was sent to another orphanage, until a place became available in an institution. The new orphanage was called Gerdahemmet Aby. I arrived there on 1 July 1947. It is strange now to think I was in all these places.

The months passed and summer turned to winter. I remained in Gerdahemmet Aby. It was a bitterly cold winter in Sweden. I was three years old. I still could not talk. No one had ever taken the time to teach me. No one had spent enough time with me. I made noises, like an animal, but I didn't know how to express any feeling. Then one day, on 15 November 1947, we were lined up in the orphanage hall again. It meant parents were coming.

I saw a man and a woman come through the door, and sit down in the office. The man had the nicest eyes I had ever seen. The matron tried to hold me back. She scolded me, but I ran down the corridor, towards the man, and stopped in front of him. He leaned down, picked me up, and put me on his lap. The matron, out of breath from chasing me down the hall, apologised to the man as she tried to prise me from his lap, pulling on my arms. I gripped onto him even tighter, and the man pushed the nurse away. He looked down at me for a moment, and said, 'I'll not go home without this little girl. She is mine.'

And that is when Simon became my father. It is my earliest memory, and it is as clear today, in my mind, as though it was yesterday. So *I* was the one who chose *him*. I chose my parents, rather than the other way around.

It is the day that Valborg became my mother too. I don't remember her so clearly, though she was there. But I remember Simon.

Simon was the nicest person I had ever met, and that is where my memory of life begins.

I can see the rest of it written down in the documents I have now. But it is as if my life didn't start until I met Simon, an adult who cared for me, and everything that came before that – Norway, the Lebensborn, the attic, and everything else – somehow I have blocked out those memories, but I know I was there, and that I lived them, and somewhere deep down, those memories exist in me. But memory is a funny thing, and because I was too young to know what was happening, those first three years, the dark years, have always been a mystery to me.

Until now.

23

Growing up

The next part of my life, the growing up, wasn't a mystery. When you have parents to tell you things, and to remember for you, there is a record of your life, of your early years, and from that day on I had parents. I was a person. Part of a family. I would have a story from then on. From the age of three.

The day Simon and Valborg came to the orphanage they brought me home with them, to their farm in Malexander, to become their daughter. The orphanage was happy that someone wanted me, though they must have wondered if I would be sent back again. Thank goodness I wasn't.

On my first night in Malexander, Simon was putting me to bed. He dressed me in a soft white linen nightdress – the one they had packed for me in the orphanage. The sleeves were so tight it hurt my arms. I didn't know how to tell him what was wrong. I still had not learned to talk. It was very painful. I wanted to tell him, to show him, but all I could do was cry. Simon looked at me. Somehow he seemed to understand. He went to the kitchen and took a knife from the drawer. He came back into the room, picked me up, and brought the knife towards me. I froze, and he sliced through the tight cotton sleeves in one quick movement. I felt instant relief. The blood was pumping through my arms again. I never forgot that night. It was the first time someone had looked after me. And I still wonder why. There I was, this feral child, unable to speak, unable to communicate. I wonder why they took me in. Why they had answered the ad in the newspaper, and why they had chosen me, when there were so many other children lined up in the corridor that day waiting to be adopted. If I hadn't run towards them, I wonder who I would be now, or if I would be alive at all.

I wonder too if they knew I was one of the Nazi-Aryan babies. They can't have known. But if they did, I wonder if they would have seen me differently, all those years growing up. All the years we spent together, if they'd known.

Slowly, Simon and Valborg taught me how to speak, one word at a time, and by the time I was ready to go to school I could speak Swedish. I would be just like all the other children.

The farm was all I had ever known, all I could remember. It was my home. But I still didn't have what other children had – citizenship. I still didn't really belong.

In 1951, at the age of seven, I was given a document to say that I was allowed to be in Sweden. It still was not citizenship, but at least it was some proof of identity. I had no other papers. My parents told me to carry this document with me at all times. I could see it meant a lot to them, though I didn't understand why. They told me that if I was ever asked for identification, to show this paper. And then one day, men in uniform came to the school and asked for identification. Everyone else produced a blue book, but my paper was different. I had it rolled up in my bag. I felt nervous, fishing it out, while everyone watched. I hated being different from all the other children.

At that stage, I had put away the memory of the orphanage, and life in Malexander was all I knew. I was from Malexander and Valborg and Simon were my mother and father. I didn't know why the teachers called me 'bastard' on my first day at school. I didn't know why the other parents didn't like their children playing with me. None of it made sense to me. I knew the children liked me. They became my friends. It was the adults who were hostile.

It was a sunny spring day, when my father decided it was time. I was out in the fields, near the lake, playing among the wild flowers. I was watching a calf and its mother in the next pasture. I had grazed my knee climbing trees and my stockings were muddy from sitting in the dewy grass. I saw Simon, my father, coming up the field so I pulled my dress over my knees, thinking I might be in trouble for destroying my good clothes.

I was on an adventure with my imaginary brother. I called him Peter. No one else could see him, only me. We were best friends. Every day we would run through the woods together, and he would rescue me when the bullies were chasing after me. We would go on elaborate adventures, under fences and into the chicken coop, and around the neighbour's yard. I just had to call him and he would arrive, my big brother. No matter where I was, or what time of day it was. That's what's great about imaginary brothers. No one could mess with me when he was around. I tried not to talk to him when the adults were there. Sometimes they caught me talking to him, and they would get angry. But it made me feel more like the other children. They all had brothers and sisters, but in my family, I was the only child. It was just Simon and Valborg, and me.

'Hide quickly! Over there!' I whispered to Peter, my invisible brother, pointing towards the tree, so that Simon wouldn't see him.

Simon smiled that gentle smile of his as he made his way towards me. I watched until I saw Peter go behind the tree, safely hidden from prying eyes. But I knew he was there, looking out for me, ready to pounce if I needed him. I wanted to tell Simon about him, so we could all play together, but I didn't know if he would like Peter. He liked me though. He always told me I was the best child in the world.

Simon sat on a rock beside me, and rested his feet.

'Hahhhhhh ... that's better,' he said. 'Kari?'

'Yes, Papa?' I said, checking the coast was clear, and that Peter was safe.

'Kari, I need to talk to you.'

I brushed off the bits of grass from my once-white cotton stockings, and tried to think of a story to explain the grass stains and my bruised knees. I handed him a daisy.

'There you are, Papa. A present for you.'

He laughed. He took me in his arms and hugged me.

'You know that we love you, Kari, don't you? You know that?'

I felt nervous. I didn't know where this was coming from. I puffed out my cheeks and kicked the dirt at my feet.

'Kari … it's okay. It's nothing bad. I just need to tell you something, something I've been meaning to tell you for a long time now. I think you're old enough to hear it.'

He lifted me onto the rock beside him.

'You're safe here with us, Kari, I want you to know that, before I say what I'm about to say, okay? Kari? Are you listening?'

'Yes, Papa.'

'Well … your mother and I, we are so happy to have you here with us. We always wanted you, Kari, we just …'

He stopped and took out a handkerchief from his top pocket, and wiped sweat from his brow. He seemed nervous too.

'It's just your mother and I couldn't have children. So, we adopted you.'

He looked at me for some kind of reaction. I said nothing. I stared at the ground.

'Do you know what that means, Kari?'

I shook my head.

'It means that we were able to look after you. Your parents had difficult times, and they were somewhere far away, and so you were in the orphanage, and we came to get you. You ran over to us. And we wanted you as our daughter, and we said we would take you to Malexander.

And that was the day you became my little daughter. It was the best day of my life.'

He put his arm around me. I didn't know what to say.

'You love Malexander, don't you, Kari? You love the farm, and playing in the fields. You're happy here, aren't you?'

It felt like the world was spinning around me.

'Papa ...' I started, then stopped.

'Yes, Kari, ask anything you want. It's important to ask.'

'Well ... where did I come from then? If I'm not from Malexander?'

He watched the calf playing with its mother in the next field, sighed and said, 'We don't know, Kari. We don't know.'

He cleared his throat, as if unsure of whether to say what he was about to say next.

'We think you were left behind in the war. But we don't know who your real parents were.'

Over the next few years, I would ask them again and again about the orphanage and how they adopted me. I was sure they must know something about my real parents. Something they weren't telling me. I think they got tired of me asking questions that they couldn't answer.

I asked Peter, my imaginary brother, and he wouldn't tell me either. One day I got angry at him for not telling me, and I never saw him again. I yelled at him and left him hiding behind one of the haystacks in the yard, and never looked for him. I was back to being an only child. I felt I could do it alone. I didn't need him anymore.

I grew up. I knew Simon and Valborg were my parents in every way that mattered. Valborg was the only mother I had ever known. She and Simon, the man I called father, were my world. They were the only life I'd known, the only family I ever had. Why did I want to know about some strangers somewhere who had abandoned me?

And maybe it was all meant to be. I was supposed to find Simon and Valborg. To make them a family. They married young, and found out soon afterwards that they were not able to have children of their own. They never knew which one of them was infertile. I think that's what made them almost dislike each other eventually, each resenting the other for depriving them of children, and secretly blaming themselves as well, in case they were the one who was infertile. They desperately wanted a child. I knew I was wanted, at least by Simon. I think I saved him in a way, and he saved me. I think Valborg never forgave me, though, for not being hers.

I wanted to belong in Malexander. Desperately. Finally it was made official. On 18 April 1961, I was granted Swedish citizenship. Finally, I would be the same as everyone else. I had the same blue booklet to say I belonged. I was 17 years old. It had taken that long. Sixteen years after the war ended, I was no longer a refugee, no longer a war child.

I think I became an adult then. It had been a happy childhood on the farm. One day, not long after I turned 17, Simon took me aside and told me I should leave. He had taught me to drive that summer, and it's only now that I realise he did that knowing I would need a car. He said it would be better for me to find my own way in the world. I couldn't stay in Malexander, he told me, because I would get stuck there, like he did.

'The world is a big place, Kari, and Malexander is small. I want you to make something of your life.'

I knew what he was saying was true. I had been working for Sven Stolpe. Working for him had made me curious about city life. About life beyond the farm. But I didn't want to abandon Simon and Valborg either. Not after everything they had given me.

'Go, Kari,' Simon said, 'do it for me.' I could see it hurt him to say it. But I knew he was right. It was time to grow up. Time to make a life of my own. I packed my bags to move to the town of Linköping, just 30 miles north of Malexander, to find a job and make a life for myself. I hugged Simon and Valborg.

'I'll visit all the time,' I said. They nodded, and waved me goodbye as I drove the car down our road, away from the farm, away from my childhood home. I watched Simon and Valborg in the rear-view mirror. I wondered what they would talk about when I was gone.

And that is how I ended up in Linköping, when Sister Dagmar gave me the job at the hospital. It was in Linköping that I would write that letter to The Red Cross, which opened up so much history for me. I could never have imagined the discoveries that lay ahead – the secrets I had yet to uncover.

24

Per

The trip to Hohehorst had helped me to build a fuller picture of my childhood. I could finally fill some of the gaps in my life. When I returned to Ireland, I felt at least some of my questions about the first years of my life had been answered.

It helped to have seen the house, to have pieced it all together in my mind, but I felt like there was still something missing in all this. Someone missing. My brother, Per.

Thinking of the story of my life made me feel alone. All the characters were gone now – Simon and Valborg lived only in my memory. There was no one from my story to share my discovery with. All these years later, I still longed to know my brother.

I hoped that he might help me to know more about Åse. Because in order to understand my story, I needed to understand my mother's story – Åse's story. It was the story of how I came to be, and how I became the property of the Nazis. Many questions were still not answered. I didn't know how she came to be my mother and how she came to be part of the Lebensborn.

I had some idea now of what she must have gone through. And it made me want to be closer to her. I still did not know if I had been taken from her or if she had given me to the Nazis.

I thought of all the things she had said during that fortnight that we spent together, to see if I could piece together her life. In the end, she had pretty much told me not to contact her again. So I never did. I kept that promise, every day, even though sometimes it was very hard.

I had to presume that by now she had passed away. I was 64 years old. So it seemed unlikely she would still be alive.

But Per would be. He wasn't much older than me. I wanted to find Per again, so that I could tell him who I was. Åse had made me promise not to tell him, but if she was dead, there was no promise to keep. I tried to reconcile myself with what I was doing. If I didn't reach out to Per, then one day it might be too late.

'Are you sure it's a good idea?' Sven asked as we sat at the kitchen table in Dublin.

'Yes, I think if I don't do it now ...' I looked at him for support.

'Okay, but I just don't want you to be disappointed if you can't find him. Who knows where he is now.'

Sven went into the next room to watch the news.

I opened the laptop and typed the name Per, with Åse's surname, Løwe, into a search engine, and waited. A man fitting his description came up on the website of a Norwegian bridge club. He was a bridge champion in his area. The name and age matched my brother's, as far as I could tell. From my mother's letters, I could work out roughly what age Per would be now. There was a photograph of him on the site holding a cup that he had won.

'FOUND HIM!' I yelled out to Sven.

'What?' he said, coming to the door of the kitchen. 'That was quick!'

'Hah … technology.'

'Are you sure it's him?'

'Look!' I said.

Sven came up behind me and looked at the screen from over my shoulder.

'My God … That's him?'

'I recognise him. I'm almost certain.'

'What are you going to do now?'

'Ring him!' I said, picking up the handset.

Sven sat down at the kitchen table.

I smiled to myself as I dialled the Norwegian directory inquiries number. Six decades of secrets, a Nazi regime, and a world war had kept us apart. But in two minutes, Google had found him for me again.

The operator answered and I asked for a number for Per Løwe in the locality.

'Please hold,' she said. I waited.

'Shall we connect you or would you like the number?'

'Oh … just the number please,' I said, scrambling for a piece of paper, stunned at how easily I had found my long-lost brother.

I wrote the phone number down and read it back to the operator, to be sure I had taken it down correctly.

'Yes, that's right,' she said in Norwegian.

'Thank you,' I said, in Swedish, but I'm sure she understood. The languages are very closely linked. And if you speak slowly, you can have a conversation in two different languages, and understand each other quite well. It's more like the difference between Cork-speak and Dublin-speak – sometimes it feels like another language, but at other times you understand each other.

It was how I had communicated with my mother. The thought of my mother came back to me.

'What's wrong?' Sven asked. 'Aren't you glad?'

'What if she's still alive?' I said.

'Just ask him, Kari, it's okay. She doesn't have any power over you anymore.'

He was right. I knew he was right. I picked up the phone and began dialing the number, carefully adding the international code. I waited. That distant dial tone of a foreign call. My palms were sweaty against the handset. The phone rang and rang. I was just about to put down the receiver, when a man answered.

'Hello.' He sounded distant, and slightly muffled.

It dawned on me what I was doing.

'Hello?' he said again, sounding impatient.

I thought he might be about to hang up.

'Per?' I blurted out, a little too loudly.

'Yes ... who is this?'

'Per ... Løwe?'

'Yes. Who is this?'

I stopped. 'Is Åse alive?' I just had to know first.

'What? No, Åse died three years ago. Who is this?'

200

I took a deep breath. This wasn't going the way that I had hoped.

'Hello?'

'Per, I am your sister, Kari.' There was silence on the line. 'Our mother's name was Åse and she had tuberculosis in her hip.'

There was no way I could have known that if I had not known our mother. I hoped this would be enough to convince him. The silence was so long that I started to wonder if he was still there.

Then he coughed and cleared his throat, obviously trying to gather his thoughts. 'Kari you said your name was?'

'Yes, Kari Rosvall, but I was born Kari Løwe.' My strong Swedish accent must have made it all the more confusing. 'I know this is hard to believe.' I tried to help him along.

'I just ...' he started. 'Are you telling me my mother had another child?'

'Yes. Many years ago. Per ... We met once. You and I.'

'What? When? I don't think so.'

'We came to Larvik once. Me and Åse. We were sitting at the table ... with Alf and Elsa ... when you came into the room.'

He was silent. I could tell he was trying to weigh up his emotions, trying to figure it all out, searching his memory for that moment.

'Kari ...' he said, like he was testing it out.

'Yes, Per.' I could feel him coming round.

'Could you send me a photograph of yourself?'

'Yes ... of course.'

'It's just … I want to see, for myself …'

'I understand. I'll send it tomorrow.' He gave me his address, and I gave him my phone number, and he promised to call once he had time to digest the news. We said goodbye, and just as I was about to put down the phone he said, 'Thanks.'

'Sorry?'

'Thanks for calling.'

I can only imagine what must have gone through his mind that day as he sat there, alone in his house, replaying our conversation in his mind – a call from Ireland, from a Swedish woman, claiming to be his long-lost sister from Norway.

And then I thought about what he had said, that Åse had died three years ago. A sadness came over me for a moment. It was very final. It meant things could never be repaired between us. But in a way, I had come to terms with that long ago. I knew that day in 1986, when I left her house, that I would never see her again. And I never did.

The next day I took out one of the photo albums we kept in the study. I flicked through the album. My whole life seemed to revolve around photographs. They were proof, I suppose, something concrete, in a life shrouded in mystery. A picture paints a thousand words. That's what they say.

I tried to decide which photograph to send. I didn't know if it should be an old photo or a recent one. I deliberated for a few minutes, then chose one of me at 24, and went downstairs to make a cup of tea.

As I sat there thinking about it, I changed my mind

again, dashed up the stairs, and asked Sven to take a photograph of me there and then, as I was now. I looked happy, and I looked like myself. I wanted him to know that I had found happiness.

On the back of the photograph I wrote the words: *To Per, from your sister, Kari*, and put the photograph into an envelope. I walked through the laneway beside our house, down to Dundrum village, and found the nearest postbox. I dropped the letter into the green metal box and went to get a cup of coffee in a café nearby. I was a world away now from that postbox in Linköping, where I had sent my letter to The Red Cross.

I went into the shopping centre, and as I sat there in the café, sipping on my Americano, I looked around at the people sitting at the other tables. At the table next to me was a young mother. She was holding a baby on her knee, feeding him from a jar. Her other child, who looked about three, was jumping up and down, pointing at the Belgian chocolates at the counter. At the next table was an old man, who wore a tattered, flat cap and a jacket which looked as though he never took it off. The colour was fading from wear and tear. A pair of glasses and the racing pages from the newspaper were sticking out of his pocket, as he rolled a cigarette. Behind the counter was a young muscular man in a black t-shirt. He had a tightly shaved head and a square jaw. He looked like he might be Eastern European. I wondered if he had to leave his family behind when he came to Ireland in search of work.

Every one of those people had a story, just like I had mine. It was unlikely that anyone who looked at me that day, sitting there in my woollen jumper, drinking my coffee, had any inkling that I had just posted a photograph to my long-lost brother, whose father had died in the war, and whose sister, me, had been taken in by the Nazis. I'm sure no one thought that.

It goes to show, you never know.

As I sat there watching all these different lives around me, I tried to imagine the journey the photograph would make from that green postbox, all the way to Norway.

I wondered how Per would respond.

Ten days passed, and still no word from Per. Then one morning I awoke to the soft thud of letters hitting the welcome mat in the hall, and then the doorbell rang. I jumped out of bed, threw on my dressing gown and ran downstairs. I could see the figure of the postman through the glass, waiting outside. I opened the door.

'Package for you,' he smiled, handing me a parcel.

'Thank you,' I said, and closed the door.

The parcel was addressed to Kari Løwe. There is no one else on earth who would call me by that name. I knew it must be from Per. I tore open the wrapping and peered inside. It was a ceramic plate. I lifted it up to take a closer look, and a piece of paper fell to the floor. I bent down to pick it up, and on it, in careful handwriting, were the words: 'To my little sister Kari, from your big brother Per'.

I looked again at the plate, and turned it over. On the other side was a printed photograph of a handsome young man, with sandy hair and high cheekbones. And beneath the photograph, along the rim of the plate, 'Per 1963', painted in blue. I closed my eyes and hugged the photograph to my chest. He looked just like he did in my memory. I balanced the plate carefully on the bookshelf, so that I could see him looking out at me.

That evening I phoned Per and thanked him for the photograph. This time the conversation was different. We were both giddy with our new discovery. We talked for almost an hour, about our mother and how she had managed to keep so many secrets for her whole life.

Then the conversation became serious. 'Kari, you know I wasn't raised by Åse.'

'Yes, I knew that,' I said.

'A lot of the family fell out with her, because of her relationships with Germans,' he said.

Relationships that ended in me, I thought.

'We never understood how Åse could ...' He stopped himself. 'But I've thought about it a lot over the past few days and I think it's time to leave the past behind us, don't you?'

'I hope so,' I said, relieved.

'Kari, you must come and visit us,' he said. 'There are so many more relatives that you must meet.' I was glad he said that. It made me feel part of something again. He asked permission to tell the other relatives about me.

'Of course,' I said. 'I think it's time to end all the secrets.'

I promised I would talk to Sven that evening, and we would make a plan to visit.

That night I felt elated, like I was suddenly granted a family again, at the age of 64. Like my life was finally whole. I longed to know everything they could tell me about my mother, and maybe even about my father.

Six weeks later, I travelled to Norway.

'Ladies and gentlemen, we will shortly be landing in Oslo,' the captain announced over the public address system.

'You're here, Kari!' said the man in the seat beside me.

We had been sitting together during the flight, and had struck up a conversation about Oslo. I couldn't contain my excitement about meeting Per, and when he asked me why I was going to Norway, I said, 'I'm meeting my brother for the first time.'

He was obviously intrigued as to why siblings would be meeting in their sixties. I explained that I had been adopted, so I had not known my brother growing up. I could tell he was excited by this, and that he was delighted, in some small way, to be part of the story. It was only when I saw his reaction that I realised how big a moment this was. How important it was.

When I walked through the arrivals hall, I scanned the sea of faces, looking for Per. And then I spotted him. We made eye contact. He waved and pushed his way through the crowd.

'Kari!'

'Per!'

We studied one another for a moment, then threw our arms out and hugged each other. We laughed.

'It's so lovely to meet you, sister,' said Per.

'Hello, brother!' I said.

We seemed to share the same sense of humour, which made me look forward to the days ahead. There he was, the brother I had longed for. I felt as though Peter, my imaginary brother, was finally coming out from behind the haystack. He was real, no longer imaginary; he was my brother. He looked so much older than the memory I held of him – the one I sealed in my mind that night in Norway all those years ago, of him coming through the kitchen door, the only other time I ever met him. But his smile still looked the same.

Part of me had worried that, being Åse's son, Per might have the same cautious attitude that she had with me. But I knew from our telephone conversations that he wasn't like her. He actually seemed to want me in his life. Though Åse had also been warm when we first met. But she had changed over the time we spent together. I often wondered if that was my fault, if I could have done something differently when I met Åse to make her happy to have me in her life. So as the taxi made its way through the streets of Oslo, I tried to keep smiling, and to keep the conversation interesting, hoping that Per would like me, that he would continue to want me.

25

Åse's story

Over the days that followed I learned a lot about my mother, about who she was. I had focused so much on what my mother meant to me and who she was to me, I had almost forgotten that before she was my mother, she was just Åse. She had a life before I was born, a life that brought her to that hospital bed, a life that brought her to my birth. I think I have a clearer picture now of who she was. Who Åse was. This is her story – this is Åse's story.

Åse was born in a village in the south of Norway called Larvik. There were five children in her family and she was the middle child. She had three brothers, two older and one younger. And an elder sister who died in childbirth.

It was a tough upbringing and she too almost died, when she was a child. She suffered from tuberculosis, and was hospitalised when she was seven years old. She had to stay in hospital for nearly a year.

I tried to imagine what that must have been like for her. Hospital must have been a terrible place for a child in those days. Her family was poor. They didn't have the money for the bus and had to walk to the hospital to see her, and it was many miles. So she had to be strong. She had to grow up quickly.

Eventually she recovered and went back to school. She was lucky. The doctors thought she wouldn't make it, but she pulled through. She went back to normal life, but she was never very fond of school, and she left as soon as she could. Maybe my mother and I weren't that different after all, I thought, seeing the similarities in our childhoods.

When she was a teenager she decided to open a café. Larvik was a small seaside town. Sailors and truck drivers often passed through, and so she saw an opportunity. She opened a café and catered for the men who drove the lorries and worked on the boats. She served hot food and coffee. From what I can gather she was very charming and they all knew her by name. She was beautiful too, and popular with men.

But then, even though the café was doing well, she started to feel restless. My mother lived her life on the move, always looking for the next adventure. She could never become too attached. Life in Larvik became too small for her, so she packed her bags and travelled to Oslo to see if she could find a new life in the big city. And though she didn't know it yet, this move would change the rest of her life.

I thought of my own move to Linköping, all those years ago. Maybe I had inherited her sense of adventure. I kept looking for myself in her story.

She was just 23 years old the year the war broke out and a year later Norway was occupied. I do not know if that made her afraid, but I imagine that it did. In Oslo she fell in love with a young man, a soldier, and before long she was pregnant.

I imagine what it must have been like for her. I imagine that at night time they would talk in bed about the future, and all the dreams that lay ahead. Like me and Daniel in Linköping. He made her laugh, too. She couldn't believe she had lived her whole life not knowing him. But now she had found him, and they would be married, and live together forever. Or so she must have thought. She must have been happy during that time, during her pregnancy. They say she was softer then. She was in love and she was loved. You think love will last forever. Before you really know pain, you think that.

They thought they would see the world together, but this was wartime and the future of the world was yet to be decided. Her fiancé was sent away, to another part of the country, with his unit. She waited for him, hoping he would be home in time for the birth of their child.

And then the day came, in January. She gave birth to a beautiful baby boy, Per. That same day she received a telegram to say that the father of her child had been killed in the war. Her lover was gone. He was dead. Just like that, her whole world collapsed around her in a moment. I think I know how she felt then, too.

She must have lain there, grief-stricken, with her new son. He must have looked so like his father. Now it was just the two of them. The joy was gone out of her life and she would never be the same again. He was the only one who ever knew her, knew what she could have been. She was her best self with him, and she would never be that person again. She died with him that day. How tragic, I thought, imagining how different my mother's life might have been if he had lived. How one life can impact on another that way. The domino effect of love and death. Like when Mr Grahs died and they took me back to the orphanage, I thought. Life can go left or right.

I imagine she was heartbroken. And sometimes people don't recover from that.

Then news came that Åse's younger brother had also been killed. He too was a soldier. Another death and still the war raged on.

It must have been a very difficult time for her. She had to be a mother, but she was suffering too. I knew what that was like.

The baby cried a lot. The apartment was cold, and she found it hard to leave the bed. She would leave the baby, wailing, while she placed the pillow over her head, unable to cope.

Then, one day she had to go to the welfare office. That's when her life changed again. They say she had become unrecognisable. If anyone had once known the glamorous girl from the Larvik café, they would have passed her by on the street that day. She wore black. She was mourning. She was exhausted from crying.

At the welfare office they told her she would need to start work. She would be placed in an office, to work as a secretary to the German soldiers. She would start the following week. That must have been the hardest thing for her.

She was assigned to a busy office for high-ranking SS men. She was smart, and diligent. But there was a sadness in her. She didn't want to be part of anything that had to do with the war. The war had taken the love of her life.

One year later she was pregnant again. And this is the part of the story she never told. I do not know if she fell in love or if she was raped. Nobody knows how I came to be. One way or another, she met Kurt Zeidler and they were together in December of 1943. That is all we know, because I was born in September 1944. To this day, no one has been able to find out for sure who Kurt Zeidler was. So there are parts of my story that will always be blank. Because parts of her story are blank, and she's no longer here to tell them to us. And even when she was here, she was too frightened to say.

So, I can only imagine what might have happened. Who Kurt Zeidler might have been.

Sometimes I play out both scenarios in my head. Either could be true.

She may have met a handsome soldier in the office who was not like all the rest. Kurt Zeidler was compassionate and kind. I like to think of him that way. I imagine that he had been drafted into the war but he didn't belong there. He didn't want to be there. He was young and intelligent, and missed his family back home in Germany. Then he met Åse. My mother. They fell in love, and slept together, and I was born, nine months later. That is the story I like.

Or there is another possibility. Kurt Zeidler was a much older German soldier, a high-ranking SS man who did terrible things to people during the war, and preyed on women. He raped her. His breath heavy with alcohol. And I was born nine months later. I find it hard to think about that story.

Either way, she fell pregnant with me.

That man, whoever he was, he was my father.

I will never know which one of those stories is true. Or if they did it knowing they would have me, to give me up to the Lebensborn.

I feel happier not knowing which it is.

All I know is that the records say my father's name was Kurt Zeidler. But even that may not be the truth. I have been told that many of the forms documenting the births of Lebensborn children were falsified to protect high-ranking SS men, or men who were already married. Kurt Zeidler is just an idea to me. I will never know who my father was to my mother, and though I have often thought about it, perhaps I am better off not knowing, because that way I can dream the best reality for her. At least then there is hope that she may have loved him. That I may have been born out of love. I will never know who they truly were, those people in that moment in time: my mother, and my father.

She was taken to hospital in Oslo. She still suffered from tuberculosis, in her hip. The birth was long and painful. It was a complicated procedure. The records show that the doctor was German. She pushed for hours. Until finally I arrived. All eight pounds, seven ounces of me.

She was exhausted.

I imagine her there, tired, and afraid. I think she loved me. I have to think that. I might have reminded her of the handsome German soldier. Or maybe I reminded her of something much more painful – of the alcoholic breath on her neck. But there is one thing I do know. I was her child. Her daughter.

So there she was, still in pain, in the hospital bed. And then they chose me. They knew my father was German, and my mother Norwegian. They took me from her, after just ten days together. The only thing she had left was taken away from her. Per was two years old then, and was being looked after by relatives. She could not cope with looking after him.

She watched me being taken from her. She had carried me for nine months, and now I was gone. Just like that. Some people say the Norwegian women agreed to the adoptions, but all I know is what she told me, and she told me I was taken from her, so I must believe that.

I will never truly know if my mother was complicit in this scheme. If she gave me to strangers, to the Nazis, to be part of their stock. Or if, like she says, I was taken from her. That is the one question I will always live with.

All I know is she left the hospital where I was born without me. And I choose to believe I was taken. I choose that. But I will never know for sure. I would rather believe it was Kurt Zeidler who was complicit. My father. The soldiers were offered rewards for fathering Lebensborn children. He must have pointed them in the direction of the woman he made pregnant, so they could collect me, the baby, the product of their union. So he could collect his prize. This is how I have reconciled it in my mind. To me, this is the story. All I know is, whatever way the

Nazis came to know about my birth, regardless of how that happened, I found myself, as a baby, in Germany, in a Nazi programme called the Lebensborn.

I cannot be too hard on my mother. I know that now. It is difficult to imagine the fear she might have experienced, because we don't have to feel like that in a democracy, but during that time Hitler's word was law. People would be killed if they didn't do as he commanded. It is hard to imagine a man with so much power over people's lives. He changed my life, and my mother's life. I don't know why the SS men did it – if it was to follow orders, or if they were paid, but they did it in their thousands – impregnating Norwegian girls, and German girls. It was about control. Hitler wanted to control everything and everyone. And he, with such dark features, wishing the world blonde. I may have survived the war, and although I was only a baby when the war ended, my life was completely shaped by it.

There is no way of knowing exactly what happened next. All I know is that this was a dark time in Åse's life. She had to stay in Oslo to try to recover. She couldn't be around the Germans anymore. She found work at The Grand Hotel in Oslo.

In 1944, the war raged on and it must have been a frightening time for her. The news headlines were full of stories of bombings and of men, women and children dying. I wonder if she opened the newspapers and thought of me. If she worried I might have been one of those children every time she heard of a fatality somewhere. Or maybe she knew that I was in the hands of the Nazis, in a Lebensborn home, far away. Maybe she didn't worry about me at all. Put me out of her mind entirely. I do not know.

And perhaps she was worried for her own life as the Germans marched through the streets of Oslo. There was danger in the air. Every day brought uncertainty. And she had slept with the enemy. The worst thing a woman could do.

So she kept my birth a secret, even from her own family, and supported herself by working in The Grand Hotel. She lived a lonely life, working extra-long shifts, and weekends. I think it was her way of being numb to everything that was happening around her. She had lost the man she loved and her two children. She didn't have the strength to raise Per. He was being looked after by relatives in Larvik, before he was old enough to know the difference. And there he would stay. It was best for everyone, it was decided. Now she was alone. All those nights spent talking about what the future might bring. She never imagined it would be like this.

She never told her family about the pregnancy. She couldn't go home for months, for fear they would notice she was pregnant. She stayed away, and kept it all a secret. But somehow, they heard rumours, of her and a German soldier. One of her brothers made it known she wouldn't be welcome back at home. How could she be with a German, after what they had done. They had killed her brother, and so many others. People talked. Larvik was a small place, and people were hurting. Norway had been invaded. They were living by Hitler's rules now, and it seemed like Åse was part of that. Like she was choosing the enemy's side.

She had been seen with German men. They didn't know the full story, and she couldn't tell them. So they believed the worst of her. And in a way, it was the truth. She had been with a German soldier. So she found herself even more isolated, wiping tables and clearing coffee cups, surrounded by strangers in The Grand Hotel in Oslo.

She had gone through so much, my mother, before the age of 25. I think she was never right after that. She threw herself into things so she wouldn't have to think. The war made everyone afraid. But she had reason to be afraid. Everyone she loved had been taken from her, one way or another.

So she decided to leave Norway. When she had left Larvik all those years before, she had gone in search of adventure – chasing something, a dream, that was just beyond the horizon. She was a dreamer then. But when she left Oslo, it wasn't like that. It was about running away. And I think she kept running for the rest of her life.

She found work as a waitress on a cruise ship which travelled the world. She would do that for many years. When the war ended, she couldn't bear to be in Norway. It held too much pain for her. And so she stayed away as much as possible.

I was taken from her, but she abandoned Per. I don't think he ever really forgave her for that. Even years later he could not set foot inside her house. He told me to take any photographs or belongings of hers that I liked, during my visit with him. He pointed to a box in the corner of the room. I sifted through her things, wiping away the dust. A whole lifetime in a box, I thought. It felt strange to see her face again, there in the photographs. It reminded me of the times I had visited her. All the photographs were of her, alone. A solitary life, I thought. It must have been very lonely for her. Then I cast my mind back to the day in the nursing home when we had visited her mother, Anna. They were close. I could see that. At least she had that. That gave me some relief – to know that she was not always alone in life. The rest of Åse's family never seemed to make peace with her, but at least her mother Anna never abandoned her. Despite the rumours of Åse and the Germans, her mother was kind to her. So Åse knew what it was like to have a mother she was close to. I would never know that feeling.

The thought made me sad. But at least now, I was getting to know some part of her. I chose some photographs of her as a young woman – to try and remember her as she had once been. And at the bottom of the box I found a delicate powder compact. I held it in the palm of my hand, as I imagined she had done so many times in her life. I packed it in my suitcase, along with the photographs, to take home to Ireland with me – to make the picture of my life a little more complete.

Per had inherited all her things, but they held no sentimental value for him. In a way, the day his father died, his mother died too. Though the battle is long consigned to history books, that bullet still lives inside Per. He exists now in the 21st-century world of connectivity and digital technology, but that single bullet fired in the Second World War changed his life forever. He still lives with that. Deep down, the scars of that war live on in him. I tried to tell him about the Lebensborn, but the less said about it the better, was his view. Nothing seemed to surprise him about Åse. And they had all suspected she had liaisons with German soldiers, all those years ago. I couldn't blame Per for how he felt.

But I was so grateful to him. He had shared my past with me.

I wondered if other Lebensborn children had been so lucky, if they had been able to find their real families again. I decided I would try to seek them out, to see if they felt the same way I did.

26

Lebensborn children

I wanted to know that I wasn't alone, that I wasn't the only one. I went online and found contacts for other Lebensborn children, and we arranged to meet in Oslo. The other survivors were very nice about it. Very understanding. But I suppose they knew what I was going through.

It's funny how I call them children. They were adults then, of course. And that's the one thing they were never really allowed to be – children – so it's an ironic term really. It's the one thing that was stolen from them – their childhoods. We met in a public place. They looked normal, just as I looked normal. And for their sakes I will not talk about their stories, because everyone must make their own way on this path, and I know that more than most. We will all cope with it differently, we Lebensborn children. But there were things that comforted me in speaking with them. We had suffered the same stigmas. The same words came up – 'bastard', 'abandonment'. It made me feel less alone. Other people had gone through this as well, though we all had different lives afterwards, and different ways of dealing with things. Some of them seemed more broken than me. But I was lucky. I had found Sven. I had Roger. Maybe some weren't so lucky.

I spent some time looking at the stories of the many Lebensborn children, now scattered all over Europe. We were the debris from the war, and in a few years, we will all be gone. So I wanted so badly for the Lebensborn children not to be forgotten. We have a shared experience unlike any other. For many, life became too painful to bear. Many children of the Lebensborn became addicts in later life, or died by suicide. I was one of the lucky ones. I survived it. Not everyone did. It was life-threatening. To think, the power Hitler and his band of bullies held over people long after they died. They were gone, but the legacy of hurt still exists today, beating inside the hearts of these adults without childhoods.

People found out in different ways too that they had been born into the Lebensborn programme. Somehow the secret was revealed to each of us. We children of war, each had a cross to bear.

One man learned later in life that he was Heinrich Himmler's godson. He found a grey metal cup in his parents' cupboard, which had engraved on it the words *From your godfather Heinrich Himmler.* He spent the rest of his life grappling with those words, and the place they left him in the world, linked to such evil. But at the end of the day it was nothing more than bad luck. No one can choose their biology, and no one can choose their birth date.

That man was unlucky to be born on Heinrich Himmler's birthday, 7 October. Any child in the Lebensborn who was born on Himmler's birthday became his godchild, and received special attention from him – birthday gifts and extra visits. Himmler had an unhealthy obsession with the Lebensborn. He visited the homes and the children regularly, and involved himself in the running of the programme.

The quest for the 'master race' affected so many people in so many different ways. In one interview, I watched a man in his seventies break down in floods of tears. He was one of the kidnapped children from Eastern Europe. He looked into the camera, and I could see he was trying to stay strong. He was trying to compose himself to tell his story, but his voice cracked, and he wept. All he knew was that once upon a time he had a loving family. He had been out running an errand for his mother when he was spotted by German soldiers. He was precisely what Himmler had described. He looked like an Aryan child. He was snatched, right there on the road. The bundle of sticks he was carrying fell to the ground as he was lifted into the army truck. And right then, he lost his childhood, his innocence. His father and mother must have worried all through the night, they must have searched every field and path for years to come, looking for their son. They would live the rest of their lives not knowing where he was gone. He vanished into thin air. He was just old enough to feel the loss of his parents, but still young enough to forget in time. He will never know now who his parents were. He will never know his mother. He has hoped many times in his life that he could return to that village, and walk through the door of his home, and tell them he's alright.

He longs to know them. But they will have died by now. They would never know their son. He had wanted so many times to seek them out, but he would not know where to start. All he knows is he came from a village somewhere in Eastern Europe. Where would you begin to look? This is the pain the Lebensborn caused. It is displacement. They are stolen lives.

Guilt is a big part of it all. A big part of all our journeys. Many of us tried to seek out our biological parents. I never met Kurt Zeidler, but some Lebensborn children did reunite with their fathers. Some of those fathers must have done terrible things during the war. How do you live with that, being part of evil? It is something we are all left with, we Lebensborn children, though we did not ask for it, nor did we ever really play a part at all.

But they tried to take our innocence from us. We were all baptised under that dagger. We all lay across that white pillow. And they swore allegiance to Hitler on our behalf. We never had a choice.

We would have chosen normal lives, with normal mothers and fathers. The safety and love of family. And a place to call home.

27

Kurt Zeidler

I did try to find Kurt Zeidler. I wanted to know everything I could, and though my brother was able to fill in some of the gaps in my past about my mother, he couldn't tell me about my father. I kept thinking about the blank parts of the story. I wanted to know if there was any way of finding out who Kurt Zeidler was.

'He was not a nice man,' my mother had said. That is all I knew of him. I had imagined stories about him in my head. I needed to know the truth.

I made an appointment with an archivist at government buildings in Oslo. I had written to him to ask if he could find out any information about Kurt Zeidler. He told me I was in luck. Although the Germans had burned most documents near the end of the war, many of the documents that passed through Norway were still in good condition.

I met him where the archives were kept and we walked through rows and rows of cardboard boxes, all perfectly numbered and lettered, with dates and places mapping out thousands of lives through time. I felt like I was on death row, walking slowly to the place where I would meet my maker. I followed the archivist.

Suddenly he stopped.

He climbed a ladder, and used a long metal pole to fetch the box he needed.

'Here we go,' he said. 'This should be the one we're looking for.'

He took the box down and checked the label. 'Yes, this is it,' he said.

He pulled two chairs up to a metal table in the middle of the room, and motioned for me to sit down.

'Are you sure you're ready for whatever you are about to find out?' he said.

It was time to meet Kurt Zeidler, my father. I needed to know what or who he was. If he was one of Hitler's henchmen I needed to know, because otherwise I would live the rest of my life wondering if he was, and thinking that he might have been, and that I was the daughter of a man who did terrible things. I needed to know either way. I was ready.

'Yes,' I said.

He opened the box and leafed through the cards inside, took one out and placed it on the table.

He studied it for a moment. He was expressionless.

My heart was beating fast. Maybe I wasn't ready for this, I thought. I could die not knowing, maybe that was fine. At least I wouldn't have another shock in life.

'He was not a high-ranking SS man,' he said.

I will never be able to explain the relief I felt in that moment.

'He was a foot soldier,' he said, and looked at me.

He smiled when he saw the relief on my face.

'Is that what you hoped to hear?'

'Yes,' I said, 'that will do. That's much better than what I had imagined.'

'He was still in the Nazi party. He was a German soldier.'

'Yes, I know,' I said, 'but I've made my peace with that.'

'I feel I have to tell you,' he said, 'that there is no way of us knowing, for sure. A lot of the documents were falsified during the war.'

'I know I will never really know who Kurt Zeidler was, but at least now I can believe there's less of a chance that he was something entirely evil.'

The man nodded. I knew he didn't understand, but it didn't matter.

He had been part of a very important moment on my journey. There was nothing to say if Kurt Zeidler was alive or dead, but chances were, he was gone. But at least now I knew he wasn't as evil as he could have been. I walked a little taller from then on. I felt I didn't have as much to hide.

28

Arnt

I thought I had a full picture of my mother's life. I saw her as a lonely woman. She was sad and beaten down by war. That was before I found out about another secret in her life. Another one she hadn't told me. When I was in Norway, Per told me about members of my family, and tried to give me any details that he thought might help me answer questions I had about my past.

'And then of course, there's Arnt,' he said one evening, as though he had been waiting for the right moment to tell me.

'Arnt?' I said. 'Who's Arnt?'

'Arnt was Åse's partner,' he said, 'towards the end.' He cleared his throat. 'Well, more than towards the end, I suppose. They were together for nearly 28 years.'

'Åse's partner?' I had always imagined her living out her days alone. 'What was he like?'

'Oh he's still alive, Kari,' said Per, picking up on my use of the word 'was'.

'Still alive? He must be very old at this stage!'

'Well, actually, he was a good deal younger than Åse, so he's probably only in his late sixties now.'

'Hah,' I laughed. 'Younger husbands must run in the family!' I said, thinking of Sven. 'I must meet him!' I suddenly felt like the gateway to my mother had opened up again.

'I'll call him,' Per said. 'I'm just not sure how he'll feel about it.'

'Yes ... of course,' I said, checking myself. This man had every right not to want to meet me. After all, his partner had disowned me, on several occasions.

The next morning, I could hear that Per was already up and about moving around the kitchen. I could smell the steaming hot coffee as I made my way downstairs.

'Good morning!' He poured me a cup of coffee as I sat down at the table.

'Morning,' I said. 'This is lovely, thank you!'

We had treats for breakfast – Norwegian pastries and cookies.

'I got them fresh in the local bakery. I thought they might make you feel more at home.' I couldn't believe he had gone to all that trouble, for me. 'And there's more,' he said.

'Go on ...' I replied, laughing. 'I don't know how there could be more.'

'I spoke to Arnt last night.'

'And?'

'He has agreed to meet you.'

'That's such good news. When can I see him?'

'I want to give him a little bit of time,' he said. 'You

see ...' He seemed to be trying to find the right words to tell me something.

'Just say it,' I said. 'I've had a lot of surprises in my lifetime, I'm sure I can handle it.'

'No, it's not that ... it's nothing really. I think it was just a shock.'

'A shock?'

'Well, you see, Åse ...'

'She never told him about me, is that what you're going to say?'

'Yes, Kari. I'm sorry. I don't know why. She just never said it to him, and I think he's a bit hurt, that's all. Shocked, more like. Or confused. He's just trying to figure it all out. It's still quite raw.'

I suppose I could understand why she didn't tell her partner about me. Maybe she was ashamed. And she was used to keeping secrets anyway. I just felt, well, let down by her again. Even in death she had the power to reject me. And yet, the whole reason I wanted to meet Arnt was to know *her* better. I was angry with myself for always forgiving, for always going back for more.

'Will we go for a walk?' Per said, sensing that a walk around the park might do me good. 'One of our cousins, Svein, said he could meet us there. Do you want to go?'

'Yes, of course,' I said.

We headed to the park in the centre of Oslo. It was a beautiful day and soon I couldn't help feeling good again. Svein told me that his father always had a suspicion that I existed. He remembered talk from his childhood, of Åse's second baby. But he never really took much notice. The children didn't see their aunt Åse. She was always on the ships, so her life was a mystery to them, and one more child meant nothing to the cousins. But they could remember the grown-ups talking about it. For some reason I found that comforting. Even though I imagine the hushed talk of the 'second baby' was gossip in whispers and disapproving shakes of the head. At least they had some idea of me. It made me feel like part of the family, in a strange way.

I was to see Arnt the following day. He had contacted Per to say he wanted to meet with me, and to make sure I knew I was welcome at his home. He said I should call him to make the arrangements.

I went alone to Arnt's house. Per had put it all in the past and wasn't keen to go. I'll never forget Arnt's face when he came to the door. It was as though he had seen a ghost.

'It's very nice to meet you, Arnt.'

For a few minutes he said very little. I followed him into the sitting room. He seemed stunned. Finally, after what seemed a very awkward few minutes, he spoke again.

'Kari ... it's just ... you look so like Åse ... it's almost as if she ...'

I could see it was painful for him. There were photographs of him and my mother on the dresser. He seemed to love her very much. She had been dead for three years. You could tell the house once had a woman's touch. I could tell she had lived there once. Even in the room you got the sense that you were only seeing half the picture. As he sat on the sofa, I imagined she once sat beside him. I could see him studying me, the way I had studied my mother when I first met her. He was searching for signs of her. I could see it felt like God had given him a second chance. He poured some tea, and we talked of Åse.

'I am annoyed with her,' he said. 'We told each other everything.' He put his cup down on the saucer. 'Or so I thought.'

'She was good at secrets,' I said, looking at the photograph of my mother holding a lion cub in her arms. It must have been taken on one of her cruises. It's funny, I thought, because Løwe means 'lion' – Åse Løwe, Åse the lion. But lions protect their pride, they're fighters, they hunt and fight for their young. Some lion she turned out to be. Seeing Arnt's hurt made me angry again.

I walked to the dresser and picked up the photograph and studied it.

'When did you last speak to her?' Arnt asked.

'It's a long time ago now,' I said, trying to count the years in my head. 'She used to write letters, but they stopped after ...'

'After what?'

'Oh it's nothing,' I said, 'just a bad experience.'

'What happened, Kari? I might be able to help. I knew your mother better than anyone.'

'No, it wasn't anything really. It's just, the last time I met her, she seemed reluctant ...'

'Reluctant about what?'

'About me, I guess. I thought she might want to be a

part of Roger's life – my son, Roger. I suppose I was doing it for him. I came to see her again in Oslo.'

'When was this?'

'Around 1986 I think … I'm not too sure … around then.'

'And what did she say?'

'She asked that we leave it there,' I said. 'She said we had met each other, and that was that. We should close the door on things. On us, I suppose. I don't know why she did it. But I had to respect it. She gave me no choice.'

'Mmm … I see. She was complicated, your mother, Kari. She was like that with all of us. It wasn't you.'

'I've tried to tell myself that, but it's a little hard to believe. She just made things so hard.'

Arnt put his hand on my shoulder.

'Your mother had a hard life, Kari. A very hard life.'

'I know.'

'No, I don't think you do,' he said.

I said nothing.

He sat me down. 'It was harder than you can imagine …'

I could feel the muscles of my body tense. He leaned forward. I turned away from him, and tried not to think about the awful things he might say next.

'She had scars …' his voice cracked, 'on her chest.'

I turned to look at him. I remembered glimpsing the scar when she was dressing.

'They …' He took a breath. 'They tortured her. They cut her nipples off.'

I flinched.

'Sorry, Kari, I know it's not easy to hear.'

'Who ... Who would do that? Who did it?' I asked, feeling sick to my stomach.

'She would never talk about it, but of course, she had to tell me, because I saw the scars, up close.'

I could see him recoiling in his seat, thinking of the brutality that men, like animals, had brought upon the woman that he loved.

'She said it was the Nazis. They tortured her. But I don't know. We'll never know.'

I had always imagined the wrongs which had been visited on me. I had never realised just how hurt Åse must have been.

'But it may have been the Norwegians,' Arnt explained. 'Women who had relations with the Germans were considered worst of all back then. You must remember Europe was in ruins. Millions of people had died. People were mourning, and people were hurting, and those women who were sleeping with the enemy were hated nearly more than the enemy itself.'

I shook my head in disbelief.

He cleared his throat again, and kept going, like he was scared that if he stopped it would never be said.

'They say women were dragged through the streets by their hair. They were tortured, spat upon, and humiliated in public. She would never tell me the full extent of what happened, but I could see the effect it had on her. How could she stay in Norway after that? Where could she call home?'

I looked at the photograph. It made sense now – the cruise ship, running away. Deep down she was still that young girl from Larvik with the coffee shop, and a loving family. But the war changed all that. She wasn't welcome anymore. It turned everyone against each other. And maybe that's what the Nazis wanted. Her only crime was to give birth to a war child: me. I was her crime. The thing she paid for her whole life.

'It's very hard to hear,' I said, 'but it explains a lot.'

'I know. I wish I could shed more light,' Arnt said, 'but she didn't tell me any more than that. She wouldn't talk about it. She would shrug it off, or change the subject. Sometimes she would just go silent, for days. It seems there were a lot of things she didn't tell me.'

'Yes, I remember the silence,' I said.

I remembered the atmosphere in the house the first time I met my mother. Over the two weeks I had stayed with her, she just grew more and more silent. It was eerie. 'I wish I had known,' I started. 'Maybe I would have been more understanding.'

'There was nothing you could have done, Kari. I knew, and there was nothing I could do. She would get angry. At them. And at herself too sometimes, I think. It was a lot for her to carry around.'

We sat in silence for a few minutes.

'Funny, isn't it,' I said finally, 'how the men either die or become heroes. But it's the women and children of war who suffer most.'

I sat there, thinking back on the conversations I had with my mother. I felt I understood her better now, more than ever before.

I had often wondered, if I had looked for her sooner, would things have been different. It is my one regret in life, not searching for her sooner. It might have made a difference. If I was younger, if I was a child, she might have loved me. Maybe it would have been easier. We met as adults, already formed by what had happened. It seemed too late in the day to play at mother and daughter. But maybe it wouldn't have made a difference. I'll never know, and I have to live with that. But I'm thankful that she said yes, that she allowed me to find her. She could have said no. So at least she gave me that much. Even that must have been hard for her, I thought.

I stayed there with Arnt until the sun started to go down. I wasn't sure about the walk back, so I said I would go before the light was gone, in case I lost my way. We exchanged phone numbers, and promised to keep in touch. As I stood in the doorway, I saw Arnt looking at me, as though taking me in completely, the way Simon had done, all those years before. It gave me chills. I had come to think that people only take you in when they are about to leave forever. I stepped forward and hugged him.

'I will see you soon again.'

'Yes, Kari. I'll come and visit you, in Dublin. And you are always welcome here.'

'Thanks, Arnt.'

'I mean it, Kari, don't forget.'

'I won't,' I said, and I walked out into the shadows. Oslo looked warmer now than ever before. The contours of the buildings looked less severe. I could see families going inside their homes for dinner. An old man passed me, leaning on his walking stick, and smiled and said,

'Hello.' I smiled back. Something had taken the edge off. I felt more at home in the city.

I packed my things, folding everything four times over so that it all fit tightly into my suitcase. Somehow it's always harder to pack a bag for the journey back, even if you have the same amount of stuff as you had on the way there. It's one of life's mysteries, like how the way back always seems shorter. I zipped up the bag, as I sat on top of it, trying to force it shut. I checked my plane ticket in my purse, and did one last check for my passport and credit card. I looked around the room to make sure I hadn't left anything, and went downstairs to say goodbye to Per.

It's strange how quickly someone can become a part of your life, a part of the story of your life, if they let you in, and you let them in. It's wonderful really – the turn left instead of right. You never know what's around the corner. We said our farewells, and I promised to keep in touch. The taxi beeped outside and I made my way to the car. I waved goodbye and got into the cab.

'Where to?' the driver asked.

I looked at the time on my plane ticket.

'To the …' I paused. There was something I had to do before I left, and I thought there might be just enough time. 'To The Grand Hotel, please.'

'No problem,' said the taxi driver, and off we went.

He parked outside the main entrance of The Grand Hotel. I pulled on the brass handles to open the door, and stepped inside the foyer. It was like stepping back in time, with the high ceilings, and the grandeur of a bygone era.

The place was busy with people having afternoon tea, as the waiters and butlers in black and white uniforms moved around the room like an elaborate waltz. I saw a waitress in a white apron serving tea to a family. The mother sat with her three children, as the waitress placed the teas and cakes on their table. They smiled at her and said thank you. I watched her, and I felt a lump in my throat. I imagined my mother there, working in that same foyer, tending to customers. There she had kept the secret, about me. I wondered if she had been in pain when she walked around the hotel. The wounds on her breast must still have been fresh.

In that moment, surrounded by strangers, I felt closer to my mother than I ever had before. I could feel her all around me. I could finally understand. I could finally forgive.

I sat there for what must have been close to an hour. The rain began to fall heavily outside. I closed my eyes and listened to the clinking of tea cups and the whirring of coffee machines, and the laughter of people, families and friends. I opened my eyes and was gazing across the long room when I caught site of the clock. I rushed out the door and hailed another taxi to the airport, for my flight home to Ireland. I had done everything I had come to do. 'Let's leave it there,' I thought, as I closed the door of the taxi and said goodbye to The Grand Hotel. And to Oslo.

29

Sorry

When I got back to Ireland, Björn helped me fill in the paperwork. I was told I would be entitled to compensation. I wasn't sure at first if I wanted to go down that route. It had all been a lot to take in. I wanted to leave it in the past. But, one evening I was looking at the photographs of my mother, the ones Per had given me to take home, and I realised that the apology, the compensation, it wasn't just about me. It was about someone saying sorry to my mother. It was about what happened to all those mothers and children. An acknowledgement of everything we had been through.

I sent my documents to be considered by the compensation committee set up by the Norwegian government. I told them my life story and how I had been affected by being in the Lebensborn. I granted that mine was one of the luckier stories, but told them I had been hurt. I never knew my mother, or my father. It was done and it could never be undone. In many ways this programme had left me with emotional scars that would never heal.

The Lebensborn survivors as a group had fought long and hard for some kind of retribution. In 2002, the Norwegian government had finally signalled that they might be open to offering compensation, at long last, to the children of the Lebensborn.

Some of the Lebensborn survivors had terrible stories about how they were abused as children, for being part-Nazi. Some spoke of physical abuse, of being chained up, or thrown in rivers to see if they would drown. Others talked of their skin being scrubbed until it bled, to wash the Nazi away. These things I do not know about, I did not experience them, but they fill my heart with sadness.

What I do know is that we were all made to feel unwanted at some point in our lives. And that Norway was a dangerous place for children of the Lebensborn after the war, and for their mothers. We were seen as the seed of the enemy. The Third Reich wanted to protect our genes, to make a lineage for the future. After the war, our genes were what was wrong with us.

Norwegians were angry at those who had collaborated with the Germans. The warnings came, about what would happen to those women who had relationships with the German soldiers: 'We have previously issued a warning and we repeat it here, of the price these women will pay for the rest of their lives: they will be held in contempt by all Norwegians for their lack of restraint.' Åse. They were talking about Åse. That's why she ran away.

The mothers and the children were seen as evil because of everything they represented. The condemnation spread through society. It came from the very top. It is reported that in July 1945, the Norwegian Ministry of Social Affairs said of the Lebensborn children: 'To believe these children will become decent citizens is to believe rats in the cellar will become house pets.' This is why I couldn't be sent back to Norway after the war. This is why The Red Cross took me to Sweden.

Around the same time, a newspaper article suggested that young boys of the Lebensborn programme would 'bear the germ of some of those typical masculine German characteristics of which the world has now seen more than enough'. Some Lebensborn survivors claim to have been forced into adult psychiatric hospitals when they were children, because authorities branded them 'genetically bad'.

I admire them for how they found the strength to fight back, the Lebensborn survivors. In their later years they somehow found the courage to stand up to the authorities. It wasn't about retribution. It wasn't even about compensation. It was about someone saying that what happened was wrong. What the Germans did was wrong, how the world reacted was wrong. At the end of the day, we were just children, children of war. We had no say in what happened, and yet people played God with our lives. We were either lauded or spat upon. In war, people are seen as either good or bad. It's our side or theirs. There's no middle ground. No room for compassion. We were seen as 'Aryan' or vermin, depending on the time and place. We were neither. We were children.

So it was a defining moment, in 2002, when the Norwegian Standing Committee on Justice finally ordered the government to compensate the estimated

10,000 claimants. The chairman and spokesman for the Lebensborn group reacted to the news, saying, 'The Justice Committee statement has shown us an exit sign from the tunnel of darkness in which we have moved for over 50 years.'

They had heard promises before, but this seemed different. Someone was ready to apologise at last. I felt emotional, hearing about their struggle for justice. It made me feel proud, in a way, to be associated with a group of people that had fought so hard.

30

Hair

Back in Ireland, life felt fuller, more complete, now that I had found Per and Arnt. But it had all been a lot to deal with. So, Sven and I went back to exploring the countryside, and enjoying the simpler things in life. I still felt young, and being with Sven made me feel even younger. I've always had a young mind, but I couldn't deny that I was getting older. My body was starting to creak, the way old bodies do, and I had to go for regular check-ups.

I went for one such check-up not long after I had returned from Norway. I rode to the hospital on my bicycle that day. I love cycling around Dublin. I think there's a freedom in cycling. You're more in the moment. You see things that people in cars don't.

I had gone for a mammogram a few weeks earlier. It was all very routine for someone my age, and the hospital had sent a letter asking me to come in to see them. I didn't think much of it. I felt healthy. They said they needed to take a few tests. When I got there they took some blood samples.

'Are you on your own?' the doctor asked, seeing the bike helmet in my hand.

'Oh … yes,' I smiled. 'I cycled here.'

'Okay, Kari. We'll need you to come back in to us in a couple of days then.'

'There's nothing wrong, is there? Nothing … serious?'

'We'll have the results for you in a few days. But Kari …'

'Yes?'

'Don't come alone.'

I felt distracted the whole way home. A car sped past me and sounded its horn. The bike wobbled and I steadied myself again, as I rolled onto the footpath. I had run a red light. I wasn't thinking about what I was doing. When I had gathered myself I got back on the bike and made my way home.

A few days later I was back at the hospital, this time with Sven.

'Kari, you have cancer.' It's such an easy thing to say. So close to 'Kari, you don't have cancer,' but it's a world apart.

'Are you sure?' I asked.

'Yes,' the doctor said.

I think they're specially trained in these situations. Clarity is the most important part of telling a patient what is happening. Because the temptation in any other circumstance would be to sugar-coat it. But you can't sugar-coat cancer. It's raw and it's painful, and it gnaws at you from the inside, waiting for you, willing you to give in to it.

'You may need an operation.' He spoke in a calm voice. Precise. Clear. No mess.

'I don't really have time for all this at the moment,' I said. Sven took my hand.

'Kari,' the doctor tried again, 'I don't think you really understand what I'm saying. This is very serious. We have to move as quickly as possible.'

I looked at the family photograph on the doctor's table. I looked at the items on his desk – the stethoscope, the abacus, the hour glass. There was no way to slow down time. The sand would fall to the bottom no matter what. That walk, through the corridors afterwards, I will never forget it. Sven was by my side, but only I knew what it felt like.

'We'll beat this thing. Don't you worry,' Sven said, and he squeezed my hand.

The rest of the world continued as normal, but my world stood still. The hospital doors swung open and closed, trolleys squeaked down the hall, and nurses rushed in and out of rooms, attending to patients. I looked at a young nurse, talking to an older woman. I might have been that young nurse, I thought. Once upon a time that was me. And here I was now, the old woman, with breast cancer. I had always thought of evil being somewhere else, stalking from afar. I never thought of evil being inside my blood, inside my body, attacking from within. There was nowhere to hide. That's what made it so frightening.

They ran some more tests and we tried to continue with our lives, as best we could. There was nothing we could do, until they told us the next step. I came back to the hospital alone a few weeks later. And that's when they told me that the cancer was getting worse. Something needed to be done, and quick, they told me, or else …

I didn't like to think how they were going to end that sentence, so I agreed to whatever they thought needed to be done. How was I going to tell Sven?

I thought about our life together, the one we built for ourselves. Here on this island: our home. Our safe place. I thought about how I would explain it to a stranger, how I would summarise my life. My name is Kari Rosvall, and I have just been diagnosed with breast cancer. I live at the end of a small cul-de-sac in south Dublin. I live there with my husband Sven. We have good neighbours. We love our home, but we love exploring too. When we can, we like to pack an overnight bag and head out into the Irish countryside. And sometimes, when the weather's fine, Sven explores the byways on his old motorbike. He knows all the secret spots. Better than most Irish people, I would say. And then he brings me there, in the car. When Sven or I experience something, we cannot fully appreciate it until we have shared it with the other; we have not really seen it until we've seen it together.

The Vee Pass – we had seen that together just a few weeks ago. He took me there – to a valley in the mountains in County Waterford, where rhododendrons fill the fields, and there is nothing but purple as far as the eye can see.

We sped through the country lanes, with the windows down, enjoying the wind in our hair, taking in the greenery of Ireland. It was exhilarating. And then we made our way home. I love that word – home.

Above our fireplace is a mural of a red Swedish train.

Sven loves trains. Our house is full of projects – model railways surrounded by parks and figurines – perfect miniature worlds with ever-blooming flowers and never-ending picnics. Home is a little bit of him and a little bit of me. A big telescope stands in the kitchen. Sometimes we bring it out to the back garden to look at the stars. It reminds me of being a child, of seeing the aurora borealis in Malexander.

The house smells like cinnamon. I am always baking Swedish treats. In summertime, I make linen table cloths, embroidered with butterflies. In winter, I make woollen dolls and Christmas decorations to sell at the craft market. And when my son Roger comes to visit, we spend hours together, laughing over cups of tea, and telling all the stories we've stored up for one another over the months. I am always amazed at the man he has become.

All the little things that make a life.

The thought of cancer terrified me. I wasn't ready to give it all up. Not yet. Not now.

I stepped out through the hospital doors, into the open air. It was a spring day. The sky was blue and the daffodils were out in bloom. Even the dark days can be beautiful, I thought, as I waited for the bus.

'Are you getting on?' called the driver a few minutes later. I hadn't even noticed the bus was there.

'Sorry,' I said, climbing aboard.

∽∾

When I got home I made some dinner – a stew. I was mixing it with a wooden spoon, when Sven walked in the door.

'Evening!' he called, dropping his bags in the corridor and hanging up his coat.

'Food's nearly ready!' I tried to sound upbeat, probably overcompensating.

'Is everything okay?' He stopped at the door of the kitchen.

He could always tell when I wasn't myself, no matter how I tried to hide it.

He put his arm around me. 'Kari, what is it?'

'I had to go to the hospital today ...' I started, though it came out no louder than a whisper. My voice was failing me. I couldn't get the words out. I could see his body stiffen. I didn't know how I was going to tell him this. How do you tell someone you love that your cancer is growing, that you have to have a mastectomy, that you have to have a breast removed? It's such a big part of life as a couple. I was scared of what lay ahead. Sven touched my face. 'It's okay, Kari. Whatever it is, you can tell me.'

'It's the cancer, Sven.' I dropped the wooden spoon. 'It's ... not good. The tests,' I whispered.

'Oh Kari,' he said, hugging me tightly.

'It means that I'll have to have an operation,' I said, gathering myself. 'I have to have my breast removed.' I clutched my chest and looked to see how he would react.

'Kari,' he said, smiling softly. 'That means I will be able to get even closer to you.'

And then he hugged me and pulled me close. It was

the perfect thing to say. I felt so safe with him. 'We'll do it together,' he whispered.

Some letters arrived in the post that week. About the compensation. None of it seemed to matter now. It was just a reminder that I might not live to see the apology come through the door. I could only think about the here and now.

The next day, I booked an appointment in my usual hair salon. I went in and took a seat in front of the mirror. They made a fuss, as they always do with their regular customers. They fetched some tea and magazines, and Monica ran her fingers through my hair.

'Usual trim?' she asked, speaking to me through the reflection in the mirror.

'No ... I think I'll try something different today,' I said. 'I'm ready for a change.'

'Of course! What'll it be?'

'I want to go shorter. A lot shorter.'

'So about here?' she asked, placing a hand below my ear.

'No, tighter than that. Something like this.' I pointed to a woman with a cropped haircut on the glossy magazine page.

'No problem,' said Monica, fetching her scissors. 'Let's see what we can do,' she smiled.

I wondered if she wondered if I had cancer, but was too polite to ask. I felt awkward, so I opened up a magazine, to avoid conversation, and kept my head down. I could see the locks of hair falling to the floor.

'How's that?' asked Monica, holding up a mirror to the back of my head.

I looked at my reflection. It would take a lot of getting used to. I looked older. Strange how hair can do that, I thought – add or take ten years from you, depending on its shape. I liked it, though. I wouldn't have had the guts to do something new if I wasn't forced to do it. It meant I could be a whole new me, and it would be easy to manage, I thought, smiling into the mirror. I tried to look on the bright side.

'Thanks, Monica, that's perfect. Just what I wanted.'

I walked out of the salon and into the crisp morning air. This is just the beginning, I thought. But it's a good start. It was raining softly. I opened my umbrella and started the walk home.

31

Scars

It was the night before the operation. I felt like I was in a daze. I kept putting my hand to my breast absent-mindedly. I looked down at my chest, knowing that tomorrow my body would be entirely different, that it would never be the same again. I couldn't sleep, and wandered into the kitchen. I made a cup of tea and sat at the kitchen table, sipping the tea by the light of the lamp. Part of me wanted to hold on to it, my breast. It's what makes you womanly. It's maternal. It's sex. It was part of who I was. You don't realise what something means to you until it's about to be taken away. I winced at the idea that it could be carved off, scooped out, that it was just flesh and skin, that it was that easy. But I had to remind myself that there was something dangerous growing inside of it, something that could kill me. And that's just it, when it came down to it. I had to ask myself: would you do anything to stay alive? And of course, the answer was yes. This was just something that had to be done, because the alternative was even worse.

I went upstairs to wake Sven. He was in a deep sleep. I sat on the edge of the bed for a moment watching him. I knew I had to do this. I had to be brave, just for one day, and then it would be over. I needed to do it for him, for us. I nudged him gently.

'Sven, Sven, wake up, Sven.' He opened his eyes sleepily, and looked at the clock on the bedside locker. It was early. It was still dark outside.

'What is it? Is everything alright?'

'Yes, yes, it's fine. I just … I couldn't sleep.'

'Oh … can I get you anything?' He sat up against the pillow and stroked my arm.

'There is something …'

'Of course, anything.'

'Something I'd like you to do for me.' I handed him the camera case. 'Could you take a photograph of me … you know … while I'm still like this?'

'Of course.'

He took the camera, turned on the lamp and swung his legs over the side of the bed. I unbuttoned my blouse and draped it on the back of the chair and stood in front of him, baring my chest for the camera. I could hear the shutter open and close, open and close as the flash went off, like bolts of lightning from the bedroom window, while the rest of suburbia slept in darkness. It felt silly at first, and then, because it was me and Sven, it felt right.

The memory of that moment was the last thing I thought of as the needle pierced my arm, and the anaesthetic began to course through my veins. I fell asleep knowing that when I woke up a part of me would be gone.

I woke up bleary-eyed to a circle of heads in blue scrubs hovering over me. I was heavy in my body, like I was being weighed down, like that 'body full of sand' game that children play. I was the sandman on the operating table.

They moved me to a ward for the recovery process. They said they were happy with how it had all gone. Operation complete, I thought. I felt a searing pain as I tried to shift my weight onto my left side.

'Oh, not too quickly,' said the nurse, taking my arm. 'You'll have to take it easy for a few days. Just at the beginning.' She helped me down from the bed.

'I want to see it,' I said.

'To see?'

'What it looks like now … with just one.'

'Oh, Mrs Rosvall … it's still very early days. Maybe wait a little while, until the scars start to heal at least.'

'This is me for the rest of my life now. The sooner I get used to that the better.'

I went into the bathroom and locked the door. Once I was alone, I could really see what had been done to me. I let my hospital gown fall to the floor. I looked at the mirror, at all the scars across my chest. 'They'll heal in time,' the doctors had said. 'It looks worse than it is.' I tried to tell myself I was no less of a woman, that it's what's inside, not outside, that makes me a strong woman. No matter what way I looked at it, I felt maimed. I had been through so much in my life, but this was different. And yet I felt guilty for thinking that, for feeling sad because I only had one breast. Wasn't I lucky just to be alive? It felt like vanity, but it's not, it's more than that. Much more. Your body is who you are. It's where you live your whole life. It's the only thing that remains constant. I thought of Åse. How she must have felt about her scars.

People came to visit me at the hospital. They brought grapes, and magazines, and strawberries. Such delicious red strawberries. I loved being looked after. They treated me like a queen in that hospital. Each day I grew a little stronger. None of it was easy. That medication rushes through your veins, and slows you down. Everything hurts. Your hair starts to fall out. Clumps in the brush. It steals a bit more of you all the time, bits of you dying, other bits of you fighting to stay alive. And you just have to wait to see which one wins, willing the living side as much as you are able. Sometimes it was hard to sleep. I would rest my head on the soft white pillow and stare at the white tiles and metal beds in the moonlight, listening to the breathing of the other patients. In, out, in, out. Different ways of breathing, different rhythms. All clinging to life.

We're all different, I thought. So different. And yet so the same. We can all get cancer. No one is immune. I thought of the big white pillow where they lay me down to baptise me, to bring me into the Lebensborn. The swastika hanging over me like a net. But where was that net now? How can you have perfect people? The idea is just absurd. We are all just flesh and blood. And even that is only for a short time. They called me Aryan, and yet, here I was – hair falling out, skin raw from medication, and with only one breast. Fighting each day. I was no different to all those other people lying side by side in that hospital. My blonde hair chopped, my blue eyes welling with tears, in pain. The Nazis protected me when I was a baby. I was perfect. Just what they wanted. If I had shown weakness would they have killed me, the Nazis? Celebrated in strength, but what about in weakness? They sterilised the disabled, gassed those who did not fit in with the Nazi ideals. And they bred us to be different. Well, Hitler. If you could see me now – your Aryan child.

And with that, I closed my eyes and drifted off to sleep.

The nurses cared for me day and night. Some of them must have travelled a long way to be there. I'm sure they must have felt tired and worn down by shift work, but when they woke me in the mornings, they pulled across the curtains, and laughed and smiled with me. After a long, lonely night of trying to sleep, that's what I saw first thing in the morning – their faces. And I looked forward to it every night. I truly think that's what saved me. That kindness. I had thought of Ireland as my home, but it was only then that I knew it was home. My home. I felt the people hugging me, willing me better.

The doctors reassured me, and the nurses pushed me a little more each day. They would say, 'Just a little walk today, Kari, to the end of the hall and back.' I leaned on them. They shouldered my weight, and when we got to the end of the corridor they'd say, 'Just a few more steps that way. Sure you might as well. You're half way there already. It'll do you the world of good.' And before I knew it, a few steps would turn into a lap of the atrium, and after that a little further to the canteen. Each day they pushed me to go further. Some days I couldn't get out of bed at all. And even on the good days, I was tired. If it were up to me, I'd have stayed in bed all day and all night, but they didn't let me fall into myself. They asked me about Sweden. They talked to me about Roger, as I hobbled down the corridor. They told me about their boyfriends, about their children, or their dogs. They kept life interesting, kept me thinking about life outside the four walls of the hospital, and reminded me there was something to go back to.

I hated to think of Sven on his own at night. Sometimes, he fell asleep in the chair next to me, and only woke to kiss me goodbye, get a few hours' sleep at home, and get back up for work again. It must have been the hardest time for him. We were adventure buddies. We were a team. And I was threatening to break all that. I might leave him on his own, to continue the journey, and I could see that hurt him, every day, that thought. I knew he was going back to an empty house, filled with memories lying dormant, waiting for the next chapter to begin. Some days he would arrive full of stories about his day. I knew he was storing them up, waiting to tell me. Sometimes I could talk back, but other times I just closed my eyes and listened. The hardest part for me was watching him walk away – his tall figure framed by the door, his back a little more hunched through the stress of it all.

'Sven?' I whispered one night as he walked out the door.
'Yes, Kari?'
'Oh, nothing. It's fine. Goodnight.'
'Night, Kari,' he whispered. He blew a kiss, and turned and left.

I wanted so badly for him to crawl in beside me in the bed and stay with me through the long night. I didn't want to do it alone. I felt like he was living our life without me in it. That was never what we'd planned.

On my good days, I could sit up and read magazines, and talk to people. Those days happened more often as time wore on, and a little more of me was slipping into the conversation, and I was sitting up a little more and feeling stronger.

Soon it was time to go home again. I packed my bag and got ready to leave. Sven was collecting me, and I felt as though I were going on holidays. I had dreamt about the way the front door slid open, about the daffodils growing in the back garden, and about our neighbours walking their dogs outside. I wanted with every part of my body to be back in my quiet semi-detached house in our sleepy cul-de-sac. For me, it was like a trip to the rainforest. It was full of excitement and colour and wonder. Even though I still felt sore and tired, I moved a little quicker in my step that day. I went to find the nurses who had cared for me. They were at the reception. I've been the nurse in those situations, and I know how good it is when you see someone made better, walking back out the door to enjoy life again. You've been on a journey with them, and even though you become attached, you have to hope that you don't see them again, that they don't relapse. They gave me a hug and wished me well. They joked that they would miss me, and the Swedish treats that people brought me, even more. We laughed together and I joked that they'd have to hire me for catering.

It was a great feeling, leaving the hospital, ready for life again. It all seemed a bit daunting at first. You become so used to just lying there, waiting to get better. You forget about all the little things that have to be done every day, but even going out into the garden for fresh air feels like such a novelty. And you promise yourself you won't take it for granted, but of course, life continues, and you start to forget that feeling, when you're just out of hospital and you feel the breeze on your face again – that wonderful feeling.

They had given me some advice in the hospital, about things that you can do when adapting to life after a mastectomy. There is a shop in town where you can buy special bras. I felt nervous about going there. As long as I didn't go, I wouldn't have to really accept that this was permanent. But when I finally worked up the courage, I walked in and saw so many other women, browsing the rails, looking perfectly normal. They were ordinary women who had been through something extraordinarily painful, but there they were, back on their feet, living life and doing ordinary, everyday things.

I started finding ways not to let it own me. I wore caftans a lot; they were loose, and nobody needed to know the difference – one breast or two. And Roger came to see me. He always gives me strength, my little Roger. Though he's not so little anymore. He's in his forties now. Funny how your children can make you feel your age. You don't notice it creeping up on you until you see them, and even though you know what age they are, you don't really know it until they're standing in front of you again. I always expected to see a little boy bounding up the path to greet me. But he was a man now. He was working for the Japanese embassy in Stockholm as a cultural liaison officer.

I had told him about Åse and about the Lebensborn. I felt he had a right to know. I worried at first that he would see me differently because of it. But he didn't. He was supportive about it, as is his nature. He was inquisitive too, and read through the documents. He said it was important for him to know as much as he could, because it was part of his history too. He was glad I had told him. It didn't change things between us. And for that I was grateful. I was tired of secrets.

We sat at the table having tea and I listened to him talking. I loved to listen to him talk. We had become great friends over the years, and I was thankful for that. I'd hate for him to see me just as his mother, as his burden, or as his duty. I'm his friend, and I can't ask for anything more. It's wonderful. He tells me about the Japanese traditions and we get to talking about respect, and how it's different in different cultures. In Japan, title means a lot. They put a lot of store by business cards, and bowing when they greet one another. There's something inherently good in that. He has just come back from Japan, and he tells me about a cultural tradition they have when someone turns 60. At the age of 60, people have completed all five cycles of the zodiac, which, he explains, are each 12 years. So in Japanese culture, this means that at 60, you are reborn. And people hold big celebrations, to mark their rebirth, at the age of 60.

As I listened to him speak, I realised that that was how I felt – reborn in my sixties. I had been given another chance at life. I had survived cancer. I had survived the Lebensborn. And I understood more about my life than I had ever done.

I finally knew how my life had begun, about those three dark years. And the end of my life, well, thankfully, that was still a mystery. And some mysteries you can happily live with.

32

The President will see you now

Time passed. I thought I was getting better. That's what scared me most, that day, when without warning, I fell to the ground.

I came to, and saw Sven's face above me, looking worried. He had his hand on my forehead and was repeating my name, 'Kari ... Kari? Kari? Are you alright? Kari, can you hear me?'

I had passed out. It was just for a few minutes, but we were both afraid. Sven helped me into the car, and we went to the hospital. The doctors took some tests, and asked me questions. I felt dizzy. I sipped on some water they had given me, in a white plastic cup. Slowly I began to feel myself again.

'Well, the good news is, we don't think it's related to the cancer, but we are running some tests, just to be on the safe side,' said the doctor.

That was a relief. I had been cancer-free for a few years now.

'Kari, has this ever happened to you before? Have you

ever fainted like this?' he asked. I thought for a moment, trying to remember back.

'Yes,' I said. 'It's happened a lot actually. I just thought, since the cancer ... but now that I think of it, it's happened nearly every year, but not quite as bad as this.'

'Every year? Is it around a particular time each year?'

I counted out the times on my fingers, trying to remember where I was and who I was with each time it had happened.

'Yes, it's always been around this time,' I said, wondering how I had never spotted the pattern before.

'I see ...' said the doctor, taking notes.

'What does that mean?' I asked.

'Well, there is a chance that this may be psychosomatic. It's just a possibility, but sometimes if someone has experienced trauma, then around that time every year, their body has a subconscious response. Have you ever had a traumatic experience? Take your time, Kari. Though it might even be something that you've blocked out. It could have happened when you were a very small child.'

I began telling him my story, and everything that I had discovered about my past. He sat, transfixed. I think it may have been the last thing he expected to hear.

'You know, there is some research to suggest that children in the care of the Nazis during that time period were used in experiments,' he said, and then seeing the shock on my face he added, 'but I'm sure that's not the case with you. There's no reason to jump to conclusions.'

I felt sick, thinking about what might have been done to me. I have a scar on my forehead. It might be from anything, but sometimes when I see it, I shudder at that word – 'experiments'. Even just the possibility is enough to send shivers down my spine. I'll never know the true extent of what happened. But I've come to accept it. I may faint every year, but I will get up again every time, and I know I will always wake to see Sven's face above me, looking out for me.

Some days when I look in the mirror, and see an old face staring back at me, nearly 70 years of age, with big glasses and short, cropped hair, I think of that fountain in Germany at our Lebensborn home. And everything it was supposed to represent. That spring of life. What a frightening idea. But that was then, and this is now. A lot has changed in the world since then. Or at least, I hope it has.

One night, not too long ago, something struck me when I was watching the evening news. The presenter reported from the national parliament, Dáil Éireann. Enda Kenny, the Taoiseach (Prime Minister) of Ireland, stood in front of his fellow members of parliament and gave a speech, an apology to women in Ireland who had been sent to industrial laundries for various reasons, including having children outside of marriage. Many of these women were still alive. They were the survivors of the Magdalene laundries, run by Catholic nuns.

Something he said made sense to me. Holding a copy of a report written by Senator Martin McAleese, he said to the women who were subjected to abuse and humiliation in the Magdalene laundries, 'What we discuss today is your story. What we address today is how you took this country's terrible "secret" and made it your own. Burying it, carrying it in your hearts here at home, or with you to England and to Canada, America and Australia, on behalf of Ireland and the Irish people.

But from this moment on you need carry it no more. Because today we take it back. Today we acknowledge the role of the State in your ordeal.'

Hearing those words, it dawned on me that that's what hurts the most – the burden and shame of secrecy and denial. People in authority have two choices: either to expose secrets and shame the wrongdoers; or turn a blind eye and shame the victims by forcing them to carry the secrets on their own.

I've seen interviews with the mothers and the children, now in adulthood, who were the victims of the mother-and-baby homes and the Magdalene laundries. It's not that different from my story. There were forced adoptions, mothers and their children were separated. Years have gone by, yet all these people have something in common: they're exhausted. They're exhausted from living someone else's lie. Exhausted from all the secrets. Their lives were changed because people in authority decided they weren't worthy, that their actions were not in keeping with Catholic ideals. These children were called bastards too. We have that in common. We didn't know our mothers, or our fathers, because somewhere along the line, someone else decided that we shouldn't.

There is no perfect country, and Ireland is no different from any other. This island doesn't have a perfect past, it is as rocky as any other country's. It had secrets too. But it is how we choose to deal with those dark secrets now that is at the heart of the matter. If you leave them buried, you pave the way for all of this to happen again.

In Ireland I have dealt with my past, and I feel I have been treated well here. Before I came to Ireland I had spent my life searching for home. In every country I lived in, I felt the authorities never wanted to know me. But in Ireland I had been treated differently.

As I listened to the Taoiseach apologising to these women, I realised I had met the author of the report he was talking about, Dr Martin McAleese. I thought back to the day, a few years before, when out of the blue, we got a call from the office of the President of Ireland. Needless to say, the call caught us by surprise. They wanted to know if we would like to attend an afternoon tea in Áras an Uachtaráin, the official home of the Irish President. There we would meet President Mary McAleese, and her husband Dr Martin McAleese.

They had invited various groups from around Ireland, and the Irish Scandinavian Club was one of them.

'Absolutely!' I said, without thinking. 'We'll be there – me and Sven!'

I called Sven at work the minute I put down the phone.

'Sven, we are going to Áras an Uachtaráin next week. You must take the day off work.' There was no debate. We were going to accept this invitation, no matter what happened.

The day came around quickly, and I woke up early that morning, though it had been difficult to sleep the night before with all the excitement. I was like a child at Christmas.

I wore a bright blue blazer, a white blouse, matching blue slacks, and a pendant around my neck. We drove up the long driveway through the Phoenix Park. I could see deer grazing at the top of the hill. I felt like royalty as we turned the corner and carried on through the entrance to the house of the President. Security stopped us at the gates.

'Sven and Kari Rosvall,' declared Sven, leaning an elbow out the car window.

The security guard scanned the guest list on his clipboard.

'Yes, here you are. Go right in and follow the driveway around to the left,' he said, waving us through.

There were people of many nationalities mingling out on the lawn, drinking tea and wine. So many colours and shades of skin, so many different outfits, so many different stories. And we were all made to feel welcome.

We were invited inside along with the other members of the Irish Scandinavian Club, to meet the president and have a group photograph taken. We filed in, two at a time, according to protocol. When President Mary McAleese came to me, she took my hand and said she was very pleased to meet me.

Then she held my hand for a moment longer, and asked, 'Are people kind to you?'

It seemed a strange question for her to ask, and she only asked me. To this day, I think she could sense something of my journey through life. No one had ever cared to ask me that question before, no one in authority.

I looked at her, the president of the country, and said with all honesty, 'Yes, they are.'

I was so grateful to her for asking that.

I moved aside so the next person in the line could greet her. Her husband Martin McAleese stood beside her. He shook my hand, and in that moment I felt like I was finally in the right place.

I treasure that photograph now, of me and the president. It takes pride of place on our mantelpiece. I remember when the photographer was taking it, I stood next to Sven, in the back row. He naturally moves towards the back row because he's done it all his life. He's always been among the tallest in any group of people. I went to the back with Sven, and the photographer set up the shot. He adjusted the camera, surveyed the crowd, and said, 'No, no, that won't work. Could the lady at the back come to the front, please?' and pointed at me. I shuffled through the crowd, and made my way towards the front. 'Yes, that's better, yes, just beside the president there. That's perfect.'

So there I was, standing beside Mary McAleese, the president of the country. I never in my life dreamed I would be photographed with a head of state, as an invited guest in their home.

Looking at the photograph sitting on my mantelpiece years later, I thought of the journey I had made, and how important it is to ask questions. If you ask someone if people are kind to them, you have to be prepared for them to say no, and be prepared for the consequences of that. By showing an interest you might give someone the freedom to tell their secret – whether it be that they were in the Lebensborn, or a mother-and-baby home, or whatever. We all have secrets. Some people just don't ask. I don't know how the president knew to ask me. It was the first time in my life that I lived in a country where I could say yes, people were kind to me, and really mean it. It was nice to know she cared.

33

A story to tell

Sometimes when I think too much about things, I have to find a way to distract myself. I need to do something so that I don't think about it, something that forces me to be in the present moment. Everyone has a different outlet. For me, it's crafts. It sounds so simple, but I don't know where I would be without this hobby. My house is full of handmade crafts. I knit, I sew, I crochet. Every corner is filled with some part of me. Last week I crocheted a new blind for the kitchen window. It took me days. The pattern was complicated. I know why I chose that one. I had a mammogram coming up and I didn't want to think about it. It keeps me grounded, and I feel like instead of looking inwards I can do something outwardly, that makes the world a little bit more beautiful. I remember when my friend came to the house and we painted the wall above our fireplace. We spent hours choosing the colours and the design. It's bright and full of life. It's a picture of a red train making its way through the lush green Swedish countryside. There are bushes and trees and cottages and blue skies. It's about optimism. It's about the sun coming up tomorrow, and the chance to be reborn.

The compensation for the Lebensborn children came, eventually, along with a short letter from the Norwegian government to say they were sorry. They didn't say much more than that. Short, and sharp, and to the point. I used the money to apply for Irish citizenship. It seemed fitting, somehow.

And then I used whatever was left over to renovate the kitchen. It's where we cook all the meals we share with friends. It's the most important room in our house. It's where we feel most at home. It's where our most important conversations happen, where we gather at the end of the day. It felt appropriate that the money should make me feel at home. After all, that's what it had all been about – depriving me of a home for all those years.

When the kitchen was finished, I decorated it with my crochet, and with photographs. And near the door, I hung two plates on the wall. One has a photograph of Per, my brother, the brother I always wished for, and finally found almost by accident. It reminds me that sometimes miracles are possible. The other is a plate that Hans, the museum director, gave me the day I visited Hohehorst. It has a painting of the Lebensborn house on it. It reminds me of that healing journey in Germany. The day I faced the past head on. It reminds me that I'm not afraid. That I'm a brave person. It gives me strength through the hard times. I know where I came from and what I've come through when I see that plate.

I still meet with a local group from the Irish Countrywomen's Association – the ICA – every few weeks. They're mostly older ladies who go on day trips together – to museums or to local attractions. But mainly we spend our time together learning how to make crafts. We share stories with each other and companionship. I often wonder what they're trying not to think about – each of them – as they take out their knitting needles. Everyone is trying to escape something. Everyone is searching for meaning.

One day I was asked to give a talk at an ICA meeting. The ICA often asks people to come and give talks about their experiences. But I wasn't sure what to say when the chairwoman approached me. 'Kari, say you'll do it. People would love to hear your story.'

'Oh ... I don't know if I could ... To stand in front of all those people, and talk ... I'm not sure I have a lot to say.'

'Of course you do, Kari. It's an important story. You should tell it. People should hear it.'

No one had asked me to speak at a public event before. I could feel the palms of my hands sweating at the thought of it.

'At least promise me you'll think about it,' she said. 'Sleep on it and let me know what you decide.'

'OK, I'll do that,' I said, carefully packing away my crochet.

I was nervous about it. It's not easy to tell your story, especially to a group of people you meet regularly. I thought about not doing it. It's simpler just to be Kari, from Dundrum. Why complicate it, I thought. I felt like I was inviting my demons into my refuge. But something in me was urging me to do it.

A few weeks later I was at the community hall. The place was packed with people coming to hear my story. 'A World War II story of hope', they called it. They called my name. I walked onto the stage. I stood there in front of the room full of people, mostly women. Some had invited friends along. I felt nervous. I didn't know if what I had to say was worth saying, or if anyone would understand. I looked out at the crowd. They were waiting for me to start. I coughed, and the noise echoed across the hall. I didn't know where to begin, so I began at the end, and worked my way back. Because this is my story, and the people there knew me as Kari, just an ordinary woman, living an ordinary life, I began with that. Once I got the first sentence out, the rest seemed to spill out of me. I felt relief in telling the story, and you could almost hear a pin drop in the hall as I spoke. When I finished, the crowd began to clap, and one by one they took to their feet in a standing ovation. I felt emotional. I couldn't believe people felt so strongly about my story. It resonated with everyone. They were all parents, and of course, they had all been children once.

After the talk, people came over to ask me questions and tell me how much the story had affected them, emotionally. I think people look for hope. And my story is hopeful. I'm not a hero, but I am a survivor. There are a lot of things about my life that I couldn't choose. If I had a choice, I don't know if I would have taken a different path, because what happened then led me to where I am now, and to all the people I've loved in between. What's done is done. But we have to stop this happening to other women and children. There are things that shouldn't happen. These are dark things that happen in dark places. All we can do is shine a light on them and say, no more.

After that talk, I went to speak at a school. The children there were only 12 years old. I walked into the classroom. The room was full of chatter and laughter. The boys and girls were running about. The teacher clapped her hands and ordered quiet. A reluctant hush came over the room. The teacher introduced me, explaining who I was and what I was there to talk about, and asked that they keep their questions until the end of the talk. I wondered how on earth I would keep the attention of the Facebook generation, all just old enough to have heard of the Second World War in passing, in their history books, but too young, I thought, to care. I looked out at the sea of faces, at their wide-eyed expressions. How would I explain this to them, I thought. And then I realised that these were exactly the people I should be talking to. This was the generation that could change everything. My message was about bullying. I was manufactured by Hitler. He put a label on me as a baby. He tried to tell me who I was. He tried to tell me how to be in the world. But I wasn't number I/5431. I was me. I was Kari. You can't let anyone put a label on you. You can't let anyone tell you who you are. You choose who you want to be in this world. And you have choices. You can choose to be angry, or you can choose to let anger go. You can choose to be sad, or you can let sadness go.

I told them my tale. I watched as even the toughest

among them turned to children again. After the talk they asked me questions, about how I felt about things, and about what had happened to me. The questions came one after another as they raised their hands and joined in the conversation.

'Time's up,' the teacher said finally, before thanking me for coming in to speak to the class.

'Noooo,' the children groaned in unison.

They asked the teacher if they could have a little longer to continue the discussion, so we continued, until the school bell rang. I felt very proud that day when I came home. Sven asked me how it had gone, and I told him all about the children's questions. Somehow it all seemed to make sense. I felt like I had a real purpose. That Roger would have been proud of me. I felt like the other Lebensborn children would be proud too that their story was being told, because this story belongs to all of us.

So many other Lebensborn children hadn't made it through. They were the lesser-known fatalities of the war. They died by suicide or alcoholism. Things were too difficult to face. I was lucky that I found people in my life who helped me to see the blue skies, who told me to look up and never to give up. Because of those people, I am here today. Here to tell my story.

34

Up in the air

Every now and then I look into my Norway box, to remind me of the journey that I've travelled. It is a wooden trunk with a chain around it, with everything I hold dear inside, locked safely away. It is my treasure chest. Sometimes when I want to feel closer to her, I open the chest and take out the photographs of my mother and lay them out on the table. Her make-up powder is still in her compact. I take it out and press the sponge against my cheek, knowing that she once held it to hers. And I feel a part of her again.

I open the albums, and see Simon there, smiling back at me. And the white linen cloths that my mother embroidered with daffodils and daisies lie at the top of the box, reminding me that no matter how dark things are, the flowers will bloom again in spring. The white cloths remind me of Anna too, and of that moment in the nursing home. When I close my eyes I can feel her running her fingers over my face, and I can feel that connection, like she was telling me something that day, like she knew I was her granddaughter.

Today is my seventieth birthday. The house is filled with flowers – sunflowers, they are my favourite – and champagne and birthday cards in every language – Norwegian, Swedish, and Irish. There are cards from Per, from Arnt, and from my cousins. We visited Arnt just a few weeks ago, and brought him a gift, a book of Irish folklore. He loves stories, and he has come to love Ireland too. We have grown very close over the years. He calls me his step-daughter and he visits us from time to time. We laughed one time over a pint of Guinness, that Åse could never have imagined the day the two of us would be sitting together in Dublin. But we know she would be happy for us, because now she is free. She doesn't have to keep secrets anymore. She can be that girl from Larvik again, the one with all her dreams ahead of her, free from the scars of war.

Earlier, the house was filled with the sounds of children and neighbours and good friends who came to celebrate my seventieth birthday. They are our family now, here in Ireland.

Sven gave me my birthday present, a helicopter ride around Dublin. It is the perfect gift. The perfect day. Sven and I adventuring together – to the clouds and beyond. I have my mother's sense of adventure. For that I love her. And we are lions, you know, we Løwes. I know that now.

We duck our heads and climb aboard the helicopter. The propellers whirr above us. Because it's my birthday the pilot tells me I must sit in front. Sven is in the seat behind me. The chopper lifts off the ground and I can feel my stomach flip.

'Here we go, Kari!' says Sven, laughing.

'Here we go!' I yell back into my headset.

The green grass looks further and further away as we go higher into the sky, and I look down at the fields below, the patchwork quilt of Ireland. In that moment I am truly happy. The fields look like a jigsaw puzzle – all fitting together perfectly. It makes me think of the story of my life. The greatest struggle of my life has been to find the missing pieces. The greatest shock of my life was to see the picture that they painted. And now, the greatest comfort of my life is to feel perfectly complete, at last.

There is a warm September sun as the helicopter soars above the Irish Sea. I watch the waves wash up on golden beaches.

And then we touch back down to earth, landing in one of the green fields. I step back onto land, and I know I am home.

One day I will be gone, and the others like me will be gone as well, but think of me in times to come, soaring in the skies above.

Remember my story, and tell it to your children, and grandchildren, so we may never see the like of Lebensborn again. Tell them that there once was a woman named Kari, and a man named Sven, and a boy named Roger, a mother named Åse and one named Valborg, and fathers named Kurt, and Simon and Daniel, and that they lived through extraordinary times. But they were ordinary people. And though their path was rocked by evil, love won out in the end, and it always will.

No one is perfect. No one should try to be. Life is not black and white. There is only grey. And it is in that grey that we find love, that we find compassion, that we find humanity.

Acknowledgements

Thank you to Naomi Linehan for making my wish come true to have a book about my life. Without her, this book could not have been written.

I must also thank my husband Sven for always being so understanding, and my son Roger for his encouragement.

A special mention to Björn Dahl for helping me with the research, and to the Swedish and Norwegian archives for releasing the information about my first three years.

And a big thank you to Ciara Considine and all at Hachette Ireland.

Kari Rosvall

I would like to thank Kari Rosvall for sharing her story, and her wonderful outlook on life and for becoming a true friend through the year we've spent together.

I am especially grateful to my family, my rocks in life – my father, Shay; my mother, Teresa; and my sister, Laura – for their incredible love and support through this journey, and for always helping me to 'see those lights out there'.

I would also like to thank my friends for all their love and encouragement.

And a special thanks to editor Ciara Considine and all at Hachette Ireland for believing in this story.

Naomi Linehan